Spelling
Practice Book

Grade 4

Harcourt
SCHOOL PUBLISHERS

www.harcourtschool.com

Contents

Contents

Spelling Practice Book
© Harcourt • Grade 4

Making a Spelling Log

This book gives you a place to keep word lists of your own.
It's called a **SPELLING LOG**! You can make a Spelling Log on
page 125.

While you read, look for words that are **INTERESTING**.
Listen for **NEW WORDS** used by people on radio and television.

Include words that you need to use when you **WRITE**, especially
words that are hard to spell.

Before you write a word in your Spelling Log, check the spelling.
Look up the word in a **DICTIONARY** or a **THESAURUS**, or ask
for help.

To help you understand and remember the meaning of a word,
write a **DEFINITION**, a **SYNONYM**, or an **ANTONYM**. Use your
word in a sentence.

Spelling Practice Book
© Harcourt • Grade 4

Study Steps to Learn a Word

Use these steps in this order to help you remember the spelling of a word.

step 1 **SAY** the word.
Remember a time when you have heard the word used. Think about what it means.

step 2 **LOOK** at the word.
Find any prefixes, suffixes, or other word parts you know. Try to picture the word in your mind. Think of another word that is related in meaning and spelling.

step 3 **SPELL** the word to yourself.
Think about the way each sound is spelled. Notice any unusual letter patterns.

step 4 **WRITE** the word on paper.
Check the way you have formed each letter. If you have not written the word clearly or correctly, write it again.

step 5 **CHECK** what you have learned.
Cover the word and write it. If you cannot spell the word correctly, practice these steps until you can write it correctly.

Name _____

▶ Fold the paper along the dotted line. As each Spelling Word is read aloud, write it in the blank. Then unfold your paper and check your work. Practice writing any Spelling Words you missed.

1. _____

2. _____

3. _____

4. _____

5. _____

6. _____

7. _____

8. _____

9. _____

10. _____

11. _____

12. _____

13. _____

14. _____

15. _____

16. _____

17. _____

18. _____

19. _____

20. _____

Spelling Words

1. pact
2. brand
3. brick
4. crop
5. broad
6. tread
7. film
8. else
9. gram
10. gum
11. dread
12. spend
13. past
14. plot
15. heck
16. split
17. sting
18. strap
19. task
20. twin

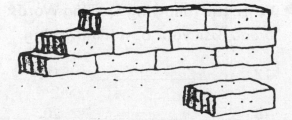

School–Home Connection

Give your child clues, such as *What is something a bee might do?* (sting) After identifying the correct word, have your child spell the word aloud.

3

Spelling Practice Book

Name _____

▶ **Write a Spelling Word to complete each sentence.**

1. I never chew _____.

2. That is my favorite _____ of cereal.

3. I watched my dad _____ the log in two.

4. Joseph has a _____ sister.

5. We live in that first _____ house.

6. Please buckle the _____ on your seatbelt.

7. Be sure to _____ carefully on the trail.

8. I want to see that new _____ tonight.

9. This story's _____ is very interesting.

10. We will _____ the weather report.

▶ **Write the Spelling Word that rhymes with each word.**

11. fact   _____

12. cram   _____

13. bring   _____

14. mask   _____

15. friend   _____

16. prop   _____

Spelling Words

1. pact
2. brand
3. brick
4. crop
5. broad
6. tread
7. film
8. else
9. gram
10. gum
11. dread
12. spend
13. past
14. plot
15. check
16. split
17. sting
18. strap
19. task
20. twin

Handwriting Tip

Remember to loop an *e* so it does not look like an *i*.

_____

- - - - - - - - - - - - -

_____ *e*

▶ **Write the following Spelling Words:** *else, dread, past,* **and** *broad.* **Use your best handwriting.**

17. _____   19. _____

18. _____   20. _____

Spelling Practice Book
© Harcourt • Grade 4

Name _____

▶ **Write a Spelling Word that is similar to each word in the list.**

1. wide _____

2. fear _____

3. movie _____

4. crack _____

5. chore _____

6. kind _____

7. plant _____

8. agreement _____

9. walk _____

▶ **Write the Spelling Word that fits each description.**

10. the action in a story _____

11. a small unit of measurement _____

12. a brother or sister born at the same time _____

13. material used to build buildings _____

14. a strip of leather _____

15. what happened before _____

Spelling Words

1. pact
2. brand
3. brick
4. crop
5. broad
6. tread
7. film
8. else
9. gram
10. gum
11. dread
12. spend
13. past
14. plot
15. check
16. split
17. sting
18. strap
19. task
20. twin

abc Spelling Strategy

Use Flashcards: Write each Spelling Word on an index card. With a partner, take turns selecting a card and calling out a word for your partner to spell. Repeat using the flashcards until both of you can correctly spell all the words.

Spelling Practice Book
© Harcourt • Grade 4

Name _____

▶ **WORD SCRAMBLE:** Unscramble the letters to write a Spelling Word.

1. tapc _____

2. prast _____

3. wint _____

4. slee _____

5. agmr _____

6. apts _____

7. ceckh _____

8. mgu _____

9. rteda _____

10. dranb _____

▶ **USE THE CLUES:** Write the Spelling Word that fits each clue.

11. something a farmer grows _____

12. the opposite of narrow _____

13. another word for a job _____

14. what you might do with money _____

15. an insect bite _____

Spelling Words

1. pact
2. brand
3. brick
4. crop
5. broad
6. tread
7. film
8. else
9. gram
10. gum
11. dread
12. spend
13. past
14. plot
15. check
16. split
17. sting
18. strap
19. task
20. twin

Spelling Practice Book
© Harcourt • Grade 4

Name _____

▶ Fold the paper along the dotted line. As each Spelling Word is read aloud, write it in the blank. Then unfold your paper and check your work. Practice writing any Spelling Words you missed.

1. _____

2. _____

3. _____

4. _____

5. _____

6. _____

7. _____

8. _____

9. _____

10. _____

11. _____

12. _____

13. _____

14. _____

15. _____

16. _____

17. _____

18. _____

19. _____

20. _____

Spelling Words

1. cheese
2. heel
3. season
4. boast
5. chief
6. gape
7. aim
8. brain
9. fluke
10. crayon
11. eagle
12. throw
13. rose
14. student
15. goal
16. woke
17. ripen
18. cube
19. rainbow
20. scrape

School–Home Connection

Play "spelling charades" with your child. Take turns using gestures and movements to act out each Spelling Word. After your child guesses a word, have him or her spell the word aloud.

Spelling Practice Book
© Harcourt • Grade 4

Name _____

▶ **Write a Spelling Word to complete each list.**

1. hawk, falcon, _____

2. pencil, marker, _____

3. cone, sphere, _____

4. teacher, class, _____

5. milk, yogurt, _____

6. foot, toe, _____

7. toss, pitch, _____

8. tulip, daisy, _____

9. leader, commander, _____

10. object, target, _____

11. heart, lungs, _____

▶ **Write the Spelling Word that matches each word or phrase.**

12. brag _____

13. scratch _____

14. point toward _____

15. stopped sleeping _____

16. time of year _____

▶ **Write the following Spelling Words:** *fluke, rainbow, gape,* **and** *ripen.* **Use your best handwriting.**

17. _____   19. _____

18. _____   20. _____

Spelling Words

1. cheese
2. heel
3. season
4. boast
5. chief
6. gape
7. aim
8. brain
9. fluke
10. crayon
11. eagle
12. throw
13. rose
14. student
15. goal
16. woke
17. ripen
18. cube
19. rainbow
20. scrape

Handwriting Tip

Be sure that all your letters sit on the bottom line.

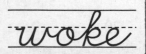

woke

Spelling Practice Book
© Harcourt • Grade 4

Name _____

▶ **Write a Spelling Word to complete each sentence.**

1. Try not to _____ about your prize.

2. An _____ soars in the sky.

3. Your skull protects your _____.

4. Jason ran to the _____ with the ball.

5. I limped because I hurt my _____.

6. This peach needs to _____ longer.

7. Autumn is my favorite _____.

8. Vanessa carefully took _____ _____ at the basketball hoop.

9. Please put that _____ with the art supplies.

▶ **Write these Spelling Words in alphabetical order.**

throw	cheese	rose
woke	rainbow	student

10. _____

11. _____

12. _____

13. _____

14. _____

15. _____

Spelling Words

1. cheese
2. heel
3. season
4. boast
5. chief
6. gape
7. aim
8. brain
9. fluke
10. crayon
11. eagle
12. throw
13. rose
14. student
15. goal
16. woke
17. ripen
18. cube
19. rainbow
20. scrape

🔤 Spelling Strategy

Proofread Twice: First, look for words that are misspelled and circle them. Then go back and proofread again.

Spelling Practice Book
© Harcourt • Grade 4

Name _____

▶ **MISSING VOWELS:** Fill in the missing vowels to complete each Spelling Word. Then write the word.

1. c__b__ _____

2. g__p__ _____

3. st__d__nt _____

4. fl__k__ _____

5. s____s__n _____

6. cr__y__n _____

7. r____nb__w _____

8. ch____s__ _____

9. r__p__n _____

10. scr__p__ _____

1. cheese
2. heel
3. season
4. boast
5. chief
6. gape
7. aim
8. brain
9. fluke
10. crayon
11. eagle
12. throw
13. rose
14. student
15. goal
16. woke
17. ripen
18. cube
19. rainbow
20. scrape

▶ **RHYME TIME:** Write the Spelling Word that best rhymes with each word.

11. legal _____

12. chose _____

13. crane _____

14. leaf _____

15. most _____

Name _____

▶ Fold the paper along the dotted line. As each Spelling Word is read aloud, write it in the blank. Then unfold your paper and check your work. Practice writing any Spelling Words you missed.

1. _____

2. _____

3. _____

4. _____

5. _____

6. _____

7. _____

8. _____

9. _____

10. _____

11. _____

12. _____

13. _____

14. _____

15. _____

16. _____

17. _____

18. _____

19. _____

20. _____

Spelling Words

1. toil
2. faucet
3. boyhood
4. choice
5. dawn
6. awful
7. foist
8. daughter
9. flaw
10. annoyed
11. royal
12. allow
13. destroy
14. blew
15. spoon
16. shampoo
17. brown
18. renew
19. wooden
20. auction

School–Home Connection

Have your child read each Spelling Word aloud and write it. Together, review the spellings. Then, have your child cut out the words and arrange them in alphabetical order.

Spelling Practice Book
© Harcourt • Grade 4

Name _____

▶ **Write a Spelling Word that fits each clue.**

1. give permission _____

2. sunrise _____

3. girl child _____

4. sell to the highest bidder _____

5. kings and queens _____

6. ruin _____

7. work very hard _____

8. terrible _____

9. hair soap _____

10. what the wind did yesterday _____

11. a mistake _____

Spelling Words

1. toil
2. faucet
3. boyhood
4. choice
5. dawn
6. awful
7. foist
8. daughter
9. flaw
10. annoyed
11. royal
12. allow
13. destroy
14. blew
15. spoon
16. shampoo
17. brown
18. renew
19. wooden
20. auction

▶ **Write the Spelling Word to complete each sentence.**

12. Please turn off the _____ after you brush your teeth.

13. John needs a _____ to eat his soup.

14. The _____ table is made of oak.

15. Emily has shiny _____ hair.

16. It's time to _____ my library books.

▶ **Write the following Spelling Words:** *annoyed, foist, choice,* **and** *boyhood.* **Use your best handwriting.**

17. _____   19. _____

18. _____   20. _____

Handwriting Tip

Remember to hold your pencil between your thumb and pointer finger. Let the pencil rest on your middle finger.

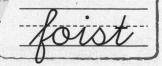

12

Name _____

▶ Write the Spelling Word that is the opposite of each word in the list.

1. repair _____

2. wonderful _____

3. sunset _____

4. forbid _____

5. son _____

6. amused _____

Spelling Words

1. toil
2. faucet
3. boyhood
4. choice
5. dawn
6. awful
7. foist
8. daughter
9. flaw
10. annoyed
11. royal
12. allow
13. destroy
14. blew
15. spoon
16. shampoo
17. brown
18. renew
19. wooden
20. auction

▶ Write a Spelling Word to complete each list.

7. fork, knife, _____

8. work, labor, _____

9. spigot, hose, _____

10. mistake, error, _____

11. stately, regal, _____

12. beige, tan, _____

13. option, selection, _____

14. soap, conditioner, _____

15. youth, male, _____

 Spelling Strategy

Word Shapes: Study a word's shape. Does it have any tall letters or any letters that reach below the line? Think of the shape as you spell the word.

Spelling Practice Book
© Harcourt • Grade 4

Name _____

▶ **RHYMING RIDDLES:** Answer each riddle by writing a Spelling Word that rhymes.

1. What do you call a girl who likes to swim?

   A _____ in water

2. What do you see when you sit in the yard at sunrise?

   You see _____ on the lawn.

3. What happens when you work in a garden?

   You _____ in the soil.

▶ **ANALOGIES:** Write the Spelling Word that best completes each analogy.

4. *Body* is to *soap* as *hair* is to _____.

5. *Plate* is to *bowl* as *knife* is to _____.

6. *Sky* is to *blue* as *dirt* is to _____.

7. *Angry* is to *mad* as *mistake* is to _____.

8. *Top* is to *bottom* as *repair* is to _____.

9. *Grow* is to *grew* as *blow* is to _____.

▶ **WORD SCRAMBLE:** Unscramble the letters to write a Spelling Word.

10. oowend   _____

11. lwauf   _____

12. actfue   _____

13. enrew   _____

14. soitf   _____

15. cutanio   _____

Spelling Words

1. toil
2. faucet
3. boyhood
4. choice
5. dawn
6. awful
7. foist
8. daughter
9. flaw
10. annoyed
11. royal
12. allow
13. destroy
14. blew
15. spoon
16. shampoo
17. brown
18. renew
19. wooden
20. auction

Spelling Practice Book
© Harcourt • Grade 4

Name _____

▶ Fold the paper along the dotted line. As each Spelling Word is read aloud, write it in the blank. Then unfold your paper and check your work. Practice writing any Spelling Words you missed.

1. _____

2. _____

3. _____

4. _____

5. _____

6. _____

7. _____

8. _____

9. _____

10. _____

11. _____

12. _____

13. _____

14. _____

15. _____

16. _____

17. _____

18. _____

19. _____

20. _____

Spelling Words

1. counting
2. craned
3. seemed
4. burned
5. chopped
6. cracked
7. begged
8. moving
9. slipped
10. sailing
11. trimmed
12. shopping
13. returned
14. watching
15. pushed
16. visited
17. cringed
18. screamed
19. scratching
20. flapping

School–Home Connection

Review the Spelling Words. Have your child point out where the -ed and -ing endings change the spellings of the base words. For example, in the word moving, the letter e is dropped when the -ing ending is added.

15

Spelling Practice Book
© Harcourt • Grade 4

Name _____

▶ **Write a Spelling Word to complete each sentence.**

1. Zach _____ his library books.

2. I _____ two eggs to make breakfast.

3. During the storm we _____ with fright.

4. We _____ my grandmother today.

5. The crowd _____ at the game.

6. The bank tellers are _____ the money.

7. Felicity is _____ to Florida.

8. The ducks are _____ their wings.

9. I _____ my neck to see the home run.

10. Carlos _____ his toast.

▶ **Write the Spelling Word to best complete each list.**

11. buying, purchasing, _____

12. slid, fell, _____

13. asked, pleaded, _____

14. sliced, minced, _____

15. seeing, observing, _____

16. shoved, forced, _____

▶ **Write the following Spelling Words:** *seemed*, *trimmed*, *sailing*, and *scratching*. **Use your best handwriting.**

17. _____   19. _____

18. _____   20. _____

Spelling Words

1. counting
2. craned
3. seemed
4. burned
5. chopped
6. cracked
7. begged
8. moving
9. slipped
10. sailing
11. trimmed
12. shopping
13. returned
14. watching
15. pushed
16. visited
17. cringed
18. screamed
19. scratching
20. flapping

Handwriting Tip

Be sure to close the curved part of the letter *d* and do not loop the up and down strokes. Otherwise, the *d* might look like *cl*.

ed

Spelling Practice Book
© Harcourt • Grade 4

▶ **Write the Spelling Word that fits each mini-definition.**

1. gave back _____

2. stretched in order to see _____

3. shrank in fear or shame _____

4. pressed or forced _____

5. gave off heat _____

6. appeared to be true _____

▶ **Write the Spelling Words that fit in each set below.**

Words That Add -ing

7. _____

8. _____

9. _____

10. _____

Word That Drops the e and Adds -ing

11. _____

Words That Double the Final p and Add -ed

12. _____   13. _____

Words That Double the Final p and Add -ing

14. _____   15. _____

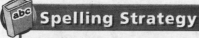
Spelling Strategy

Spelling Rules: When adding -ed or -ing to a base word with a short vowel sound and a single final consonant, the consonant is doubled before adding the ending. When the base word has a long vowel sound, the final consonant is not doubled.

Name _____

▶ **RHYME TIME: Write the Spelling Word that rhymes with each word.**

1. trailing _____

2. dropping _____

3. hinged _____

4. napping _____

5. quipped _____

6. tracked _____

7. pegged _____

8. flopped _____

9. dimmed _____

10. patching _____

▶ **OPPOSITES: Write the Spelling Word that is the opposite of each word or phrase.**

11. whispered _____

12. staying in one place _____

13. kept _____

14. pulled _____

15. stayed away from _____

Spelling Words

1. counting
2. craned
3. seemed
4. burned
5. chopped
6. cracked
7. begged
8. moving
9. slipped
10. sailing
11. trimmed
12. shopping
13. returned
14. watching
15. pushed
16. visited
17. cringed
18. screamed
19. scratching
20. flapping

18

Spelling Practice Book
© Harcourt • Grade 4

Name _____

▶ Write the missing vowels to complete the Spelling Words. Then write the words.

1. tr____d _____

2. spl__t _____

3. br____d _____

▶ Find and circle ten Spelling Words in the puzzle. Then write the words on the lines below.

c	l	s	c	r	a	p	e	h	g	o	a	l	o	s	r
h	w	e	n	e	r	e	t	u	r	n	e	d	e	y	e
i	g	p	e	o	h	c	p	a	b	r	a	i	n	r	n
e	f	l	a	w	t	b	o	y	h	o	o	d	t	a	e
f	c	h	o	i	c	e	h	c	h	o	p	p	e	d	w

4. _____   5. _____

6. _____   7. _____

8. _____   9. _____

10. _____   11. _____

12. _____   13. _____

Spelling Words

1. tread
2. broad
3. split
4. chief
5. season
6. brain
7. throw
8. goal
9. scrape
10. choice
11. allow
12. auction
13. flaw
14. daughter
15. destroy
16. renew
17. boyhood
18. returned
19. chopped
20. counting

▶ Write the Spelling Word that best completes each analogy.

14. *Swim* is to *pool* as *bid* is to _____.

15. *Aunt* is to *uncle* as _____ is to *son*.

16. *Dig* is to *shovel* as _____ is to *ball*.

17. *Run* is to *running* as *count* is to _____.

18. *Fall* is to _____ as *Thanksgiving* is to *holiday*.

19. *Leave* is to *stay* as *forbid* is to _____.

20. *Build* is to *create* as *ruin* is to _____.

19

Name _____

▶ **Unscramble the letters to write a Spelling Word.**

1. earcps   _____

2. hcife   _____

3. loga   _____

4. wthor   _____

5. essnao   _____

6. rinab   _____

▶ **Perform the math operation to write a Spelling Word.**

7. t + breath – b – th + d =   _____

8. ch + voice – v =   _____

9. f + claw – c =   _____

10. fall – f + ow =   _____

11. sp + light – gh =   _____

12. country – ry + ing =   _____

▶ **Fill in the Spelling Words to complete the word chain.**

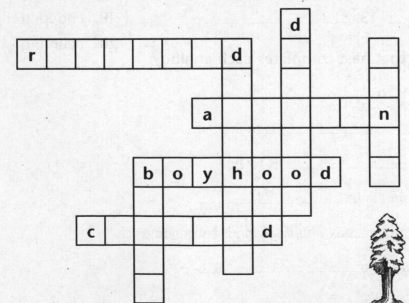

Spelling Words

1. tread
2. broad
3. split
4. chief
5. season
6. brain
7. throw
8. goal
9. scrape
10. choice
11. allow
12. auction
13. flaw
14. daughter
15. destroy
16. renew
17. boyhood
18. returned
19. chopped
20. counting

Spelling Practice Book
© Harcourt • Grade 4

Name _____

▶ **Use Spelling Words to solve the puzzle.**

ACROSS

3. a fast-paced sale
5. mistake
7. _____ your library books
8. wipe out

DOWN

1. a girl child
2. a man's youth
4. the _____ is yours
6. give permission

Spelling Words

1. tread
2. broad
3. split
4. chief
5. season
6. brain
7. throw
8. goal
9. scrape
10. choice
11. allow
12. auction
13. flaw
14. daughter
15. destroy
16. renew
17. boyhood
18. returned
19. chopped
20. counting

▶ **Write the Spelling Words that contain these smaller words.**

9. hop _____
10. son _____
11. rain _____
12. turn _____
13. row _____
14. read _____

▶ **Write the Spelling Word that rhymes with each word.**

15. leaf _____
16. pole _____
17. drape _____
18. knit _____
19. clawed _____
20. mounting _____

21

Spelling Practice Book
© Harcourt • Grade 4

Name _____

▶ Inside each word shape, write the Spelling Word that fits.

1. ☐☐☐☐☐☐☐☐

2. ☐☐☐☐☐☐☐

3. ☐☐☐☐☐☐☐

Spelling Words

1. tread
2. broad
3. split
4. chief
5. season
6. brain
7. throw
8. goal
9. scrape
10. choice
11. allow
12. auction
13. flaw
14. daughter
15. destroy
16. renew
17. boyhood
18. returned
19. chopped
20. counting

▶ Finish each phrase with a Spelling Word that rhymes.

4. new knowledge   a _____ gain

5. leader of pickpockets   a _____ thief

6. the large target   the whole _____

7. carve a figure   _____ a shape

8. wide-mouthed shark   _____ jawed shark

9. an unhurried toss   a slow _____

10. say which you want   voice your _____

11. a legal error   a law's _____

12. to permit right away   to _____ now

▶ Write the Spelling Word that fits each mini-definition.

13. yearly climate changes _____

14. a fast-paced sale _____

15. a female child _____

16. to make like new _____

17. to demolish _____

18. a man's youth _____

19. dividing evenly _____

20. to walk _____

Spelling Practice Book
© Harcourt • Grade 4

Name _____

▶ Fold the paper along the dotted line. As each Spelling
Word is read aloud, write it in the blank. Then unfold
your paper and check your work. Practice writing any
Spelling Words you missed.

1. _____

2. _____

3. _____

4. _____

5. _____

6. _____

7. _____

8. _____

9. _____

10. _____

11. _____

12. _____

13. _____

14. _____

15. _____

16. _____

17. _____

18. _____

19. _____

20. _____

Spelling Words

1. circle
2. angle
3. cradle
4. ladle
5. castle
6. ruffle
7. juggle
8. ankle
9. battle
10. candle
11. fable
12. riddle
13. icicle
14. sparkle
15. jungle
16. tangle
17. marble
18. sizzle
19. paddle
20. handle

🚌 **School–Home Connection**

Play "Spelling Word Concentration." Using
index cards, have your child write each Spelling
Word twice. Place the cards face down. Take
turns choosing two cards, spelling the word on
each card.

23

Spelling Practice Book
© Harcourt • Grade 4

Name _____

► **Write a Spelling Word to replace the underlined word or words.**

We were in the **(1)** <u>tropical forest</u>. As scientists, we were trying to solve a **(2)** <u>mystery</u> of nature. As we sat in a **(3)** <u>ring</u>, we could hear birds shrieking to each other. One small monkey, in its treetop **(4)** <u>crib</u>, watched us. Through the **(5)** <u>jumble</u> of vines, we could see the amazing stars **(6)** <u>flicker</u>.

1. _____   4. _____

2. _____   5. _____

3. _____   6. _____

► **Write the Spelling Word that fits each clue.**

7. a fight _____

8. used for light _____

9. frying sound _____

10. hold on to this _____

11. a sharp corner _____

12. frozen water _____

13. a story _____

14. to toss several things at once _____

15. a massive protected building _____

16. used to serve soup _____

► **Write the following Spelling Words:** *marble, ruffle, paddle,* **and** *ankle.* **Use your best handwriting.**

17. _____   19. _____

18. _____   20. _____

Spelling Words

1. circle
2. angle
3. cradle
4. ladle
5. castle
6. ruffle
7. juggle
8. ankle
9. battle
10. candle
11. fable
12. riddle
13. icicle
14. sparkle
15. jungle
16. tangle
17. marble
18. sizzle
19. paddle
20. handle

Handwriting Tip

Be sure that all your letters slant in the same direction.

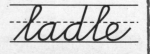

ladle

Spelling Practice Book
© Harcourt • Grade 4

Name _____

▶ Read each Spelling Word. Then sort and write the words where they belong.

Words that end in -*dle*

1. _____

2. _____

3. _____

4. _____

5. _____

6. _____

Words that end in -*gle*

7. _____

8. _____

9. _____

10. _____

▶ Write these Spelling Words in alphabetical order.

| castle | fable | icicle |
| marble | circle | |

11. _____ 14. _____

12. _____ 15. _____

13. _____

Spelling Words

1. circle
2. angle
3. cradle
4. ladle
5. castle
6. ruffle
7. juggle
8. ankle
9. battle
10. candle
11. fable
12. riddle
13. icicle
14. sparkle
15. jungle
16. tangle
17. marble
18. sizzle
19. paddle
20. handle

Spelling Strategy

Comparing Spellings: When you see a word that looks misspelled, try writing it another way. Use a dictionary to see which spelling is correct.

Spelling Practice Book
© Harcourt • Grade 4

▶ **SOLVE THE PUZZLE:** Use Spelling Words to solve the puzzle.

ACROSS

3. toss several balls
5. a fierce contest
8. a baby's bed
10. a hissing sound
11. "The Ant and the Grasshopper"

DOWN

1. _____ his feathers
2. a knotted mess
4. a small glass ball
6. hold on to
7. where royalty lives
9. a long-handled spoon

Spelling Words

1. circle
2. angle
3. cradle
4. ladle
5. castle
6. ruffle
7. juggle
8. ankle
9. battle
10. candle
11. fable
12. riddle
13. icicle
14. sparkle
15. jungle
16. tangle
17. marble
18. sizzle
19. paddle
20. handle

▶ **ANALOGIES:** Write the Spelling Word that best completes each analogy.

12. *Cube* is to *square* as *sphere* is to _____.

13. *Swing* is to *bat* as *row* is to _____.

14. *Hand* is to *wrist* as *foot* is to _____.

15. *Grass* is to *prairie* as *tree* is to _____.

Name _____

▶ Fold the paper along the dotted line. As each Spelling Word is read aloud, write it in the blank. Then unfold your paper and check your work. Practice writing any Spelling Words you missed.

1. _____
2. _____
3. _____
4. _____
5. _____
6. _____
7. _____
8. _____
9. _____
10. _____
11. _____
12. _____
13. _____
14. _____
15. _____
16. _____
17. _____
18. _____
19. _____
20. _____

Spelling Words

1. letter
2. ladder
3. appear
4. lesson
5. soccer
6. classic
7. hollow
8. supper
9. accent
10. pizza
11. officer
12. lettuce
13. better
14. slipper
15. bottom
16. ribbon
17. summer
18. college
19. occur
20. rabbit

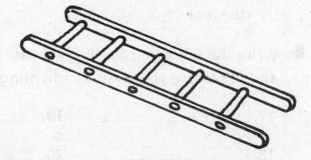

School–Home Connection

Draw ten columns on a sheet of paper. Label the columns as follows: *bb, cc, dd, ff, ll, mm, pp, ss, tt,* and *zz.* Help your child write each Spelling Word in the correct column.

Spelling Practice Book

Name _____

▶ Write a Spelling Word to complete each list.

1. football, hockey, _____

2. winter, spring, _____

3. mouse, squirrel, _____

4. sandal, shoe, _____

5. top, side, _____

6. breakfast, lunch, _____

7. carrot, tomato, _____

8. unit, chapter, _____

9. empty, open, _____

10. note, write, _____

Spelling Words

1. letter
2. ladder
3. appear
4. lesson
5. soccer
6. classic
7. hollow
8. supper
9. accent
10. pizza
11. officer
12. lettuce
13. better
14. slipper
15. bottom
16. ribbon
17. summer
18. college
19. occur
20. rabbit

▶ Write a Spelling Word to complete each sentence.

11. Ella hopes to _____ in the movies someday.

12. We need _____ to make a bow.

13. Would you like _____ for lunch?

14. That police _____ has a dog.

15. From Andy's _____, I can tell he's from England.

16. My father climbed a _____ to reach the roof.

▶ Write the following Spelling Words: *college, classic, better,* and *occur.* Use your best handwriting.

17. _____   19. _____

18. _____   20. _____

Handwriting Tip

Be sure to leave enough space between double letters.

_____

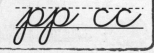

28

Name _____

▶ Write the Spelling Word that matches each word or phrase.

1. base or floor _____

2. bunny _____

3. show up or seem _____

4. warm months _____

5. salad _____

6. alphabet _____

7. decoration or award _____

8. meal _____

9. happen _____

10. improved _____

11. foot sport _____

12. house shoe _____

13. use to get higher up _____

▶ Write the Spelling Word that rhymes with each word.

14. knowledge _____

15. follow _____

Spelling Words

1. letter
2. ladder
3. appear
4. lesson
5. soccer
6. classic
7. hollow
8. supper
9. accent
10. pizza
11. officer
12. lettuce
13. better
14. slipper
15. bottom
16. ribbon
17. summer
18. college
19. occur
20. rabbit

Spelling Strategy

Say It Aloud: When you are unsure of the spelling of a two-syllable word, say the word aloud. Listen carefully to the way each syllable sounds.

Spelling Practice Book
© Harcourt • Grade 4

Name _____

▶ **MIX AND MATCH: Rearrange the syllables to write two Spelling Words.**

son bon rib les   1. _____

                   2. _____

of fi oc cer cur   3. _____

                   4. _____

cent ac ter let   5. _____

                   6. _____

ap piz pear za   7. _____

                   8. _____

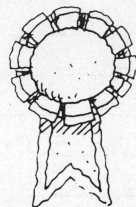

Spelling Words

1. letter
2. ladder
3. appear
4. lesson
5. soccer
6. classic
7. hollow
8. supper
9. accent
10. pizza
11. officer
12. lettuce
13. better
14. slipper
15. bottom
16. ribbon
17. summer
18. college
19. occur
20. rabbit

▶ **MISSING LETTERS: Write the missing letters to complete the Spelling Words. Then write the words.**

9. s__c____r   _____

10. sl____p__r   _____

11. l__t____c__   _____

12. h____l__w   _____

13. la_____r   _____

▶ **WORD SHAPES: Inside each word shape, write the Spelling Word that fits.**

14.

15. ⬜⬜⬜⬜⬜⬜⬜

30

Spelling Practice Book
© Harcourt • Grade 4

Name _____

▶ Fold the paper along the dotted line. As each Spelling Word is read aloud, write it in the blank. Then unfold your paper and check your work. Practice writing any Spelling Words you missed.

1. _____
2. _____
3. _____
4. _____
5. _____
6. _____
7. _____
8. _____
9. _____
10. _____
11. _____
12. _____
13. _____
14. _____
15. _____
16. _____
17. _____
18. _____
19. _____
20. _____

Spelling Words

1. history
2. number
3. hunger
4. company
5. window
6. welcome
7. blanket
8. perhaps
9. service
10. subject
11. thunder
12. furnish
13. jersey
14. mother
15. secret
16. harvest
17. winter
18. problem
19. chapter
20. nurses

School–Home Connection

On a lined sheet of paper, have your child write each Spelling Word, and carefully outline each word. Have your child pay special attention to tall letters or those that fall below the line.

31

Name _____

▶ **Write a Spelling Word that matches each mini-definition.**

1. office or business _____

2. opening in a wall _____

3. job or good deed _____

4. record of important events _____

5. greet or invite _____

6. bedcovering or layer _____

7. topic or area of study _____

8. healthcare workers _____

9. need to eat _____

10. a loud sound _____

Spelling Words

1. history
2. number
3. hunger
4. company
5. window
6. welcome
7. blanket
8. perhaps
9. service
10. subject
11. thunder
12. furnish
13. jersey
14. mother
15. secret
16. harvest
17. winter
18. problem
19. chapter
20. nurses

▶ **Write the Spelling Word that is the opposite of each word.**

11. summer _____

12. solution _____

13. certainly _____

14. letter _____

15. plant _____

16. well-known _____

Handwriting Tip

Use an overcurve stroke when you join a letter to a circle-stroke letter. Then retrace part of the circle stroke.

mo

▶ **Write the following Spelling Words:** *mother, jersey, chapter,* **and** *furnish.* **Use your best handwriting.**

17. _____   19. _____

18. _____   20. _____

Spelling Practice Book
© Harcourt • Grade 4

Name _____

▶ **Write the Spelling Word that completes each sentence.**

1. I have one more _____ of this book to read.

2. How would you like to _____ your room?

3. There's a breeze blowing through the _____ .

4. After hiking, we had a _____ for a warm meal.

5. My _____ likes to read at night.

6. This year the _____ was plentiful.

7. The _____ in that hospital are very nice.

8. Please help Ira with the math _____ .

9. My report is about the _____ of baseball.

10. I wrapped up in a soft _____ .

▶ **Write the Spelling Word that completes each phrase.**

11. _____ wonderland

12. _____ password

13. You're _____ one.

14. a warm _____

15. _____ and lightning

Spelling Words

1. history
2. number
3. hunger
4. company
5. window
6. welcome
7. blanket
8. perhaps
9. service
10. subject
11. thunder
12. furnish
13. jersey
14. mother
15. secret
16. harvest
17. winter
18. problem
19. chapter
20. nurses

 Spelling Strategy

Rhyming Words: To spell a word, write a word that rhymes with it. Then try spelling the rhyming parts the same way.

Spelling Practice Book
© Harcourt • Grade 4

Name _____

▶ **WORD OPERATIONS: Perform the math operation to write a Spelling Word.**

1. companion – ion + y = _____

2. furniture – ture + sh = _____

3. hi + store – e + y = _____

4. har + invest – in = _____

5. mo + lather – la = _____

6. su + object – o = _____

7. j + verse – v + y = _____

8. serve – e + ice = _____

9. the – e + under = _____

▶ **RHYMING RIDDLES: Answer each riddle by writing a Spelling Word that rhymes.**

10. What are bags full of bandages and medicines?

    purses for _____

11. What cowboys may wear.

    chaps, _____

12. What do you call a sleepy digit?

    a slumber _____

13. What do you call someone who runs in the snow?

    a _____ sprinter

14. What is a baby's appetite?

    a younger _____

15. What is an unhappy hello?

    a glum _____

Spelling Words

1. history
2. number
3. hunger
4. company
5. window
6. welcome
7. blanket
8. perhaps
9. service
10. subject
11. thunder
12. furnish
13. jersey
14. mother
15. secret
16. harvest
17. winter
18. problem
19. chapter
20. nurses

34

Name _____

Fold the paper along the dotted line. As each Spelling Word is read aloud, write it in the blank. Then unfold your paper and check your work. Practice writing any Spelling Words you missed.

1. _____

2. _____

3. _____

4. _____

5. _____

6. _____

7. _____

8. _____

9. _____

10. _____

11. _____

12. _____

13. _____

14. _____

15. _____

16. _____

17. _____

18. _____

19. _____

20. _____

Spelling Words

1. monster
2. complete
3. hundred
4. exchange
5. sandwich
6. surprise
7. applause
8. although
9. conflict
10. mattress
11. purchase
12. merchant
13. pumpkin
14. angry
15. Thursday
16. ostrich
17. punctual
18. address
19. chestnut
20. luncheon

Spelling Practice
© Harcourt •

Name _____

► Write a Spelling Word that is similar to each given word.

1. argument _____

2. whole _____

3. buy _____

4. mad _____

5. shock _____

6. clapping _____

7. bed _____

8. shopkeeper _____

9. on time _____

10. meal _____

Spelling Words

1. monster
2. complete
3. hundred
4. exchange
5. sandwich
6. surprise
7. applause
8. although
9. conflict
10. mattress
11. purchase
12. merchant
13. pumpkin
14. angry
15. Thursday
16. ostrich
17. punctual
18. address
19. chestnut
20. luncheon

► Write a Spelling Word to complete each sentence.

11. Dad ate two pieces of _____ pie!

12. Please write the _____ on the envelope.

13. We will see the play on _____ night.

14. This turkey _____ is delicious.

15. I want to _____ this red shirt for a green one.

16. There are a _____ pennies in one dollar.

► Write the following Spelling Words: *chestnut, ostrich, although,* and *monster*. Use your best handwriting.

17. _____   19. _____

18. _____   20. _____

Handwriting Tip

Be sure that all of your short letters are the same height.

_____

ace

36

Spelling Practice Book
© Harcourt • Grade 4

Name _____

▶ **Write a Spelling Word to complete each list.**

1. swap, replace, _____

2. fight, disagreement, _____

3. soup, salad, _____

4. obtain, money, _____

5. Tuesday, Wednesday, _____

6. name, phone number, _____

7. mean, huge, _____

8. walnut, pecan, _____

9. finish, done, _____

10. brunch, buffet, _____

11. gourd, squash, _____

Spelling Words

1. monster
2. complete
3. hundred
4. exchange
5. sandwich
6. surprise
7. applause
8. although
9. conflict
10. mattress
11. purchase
12. merchant
13. pumpkin
14. angry
15. Thursday
16. ostrich
17. punctual
18. address
19. chestnut
20. luncheon

▶ **Write the Spelling Word that completes each phrase.**

Dear Mandy,

   Today I had a big (12) shock. We went to the zoo, and I saw an (13) unusual bird. It came to me when I called, (14) even though it had never seen me before. I took pictures. I'll bring them to your house, and I promise to be (15) on time so we can play!

Your friend, Jessica

12. _____   14. _____

13. _____   15. _____

📖 **Spelling Strategy**

Using a Dictionary: If you need help deciding if a word is spelled correctly, use a dictionary.

Spelling Practice
© Harcourt

▶ **MATCH SYLLABLES: Draw a line from a syllable on the left to the one on the right to complete a Spelling Word. Then write the words.**

Spelling Words

1. ad	a. plause	_____
2. mat	b. chant	_____
3. pump	c. dress	_____
4. ex	d. prise	_____
5. chest	e. chase	_____
6. ap	f. nut	_____
7. sur	g. change	_____
8. mer	h. kin	_____
9. pur	i. tress	_____

1. monster
2. complete
3. hundred
4. exchange
5. sandwich
6. surprise
7. applause
8. although
9. conflict
10. mattress
11. purchase
12. merchant
13. pumpkin
14. angry
15. Thursday
16. ostrich
17. punctual
18. address
19. chestnut
20. luncheon

▶ **USE THE CLUES: Write the Spelling Word that fits each clue. Then use the letters in boxes to complete the riddle.**

10. not late _____ ☐_____

11. a midday meal _____ ☐

12. even if _____ ☐

13. ten times ten _____ ☐

14. day of the week _____ ☐

15. What do you call an insect that is buzzing mad?

an _____ bumblebee

Name _____

▶ **Write the Spelling Word that fits each clue.**

1. similar to a folktale _____

2. where a king lives _____

3. used to hold a pan _____

4. a strip of cloth used for decoration _____

5. frozen water that hangs down _____

▶ **Write the Spelling Word that fits each clue. Then unscramble the letters in the boxes to answer the riddle.**

6. something to be solved ☐ _____

7. female parent _____ ☐ _____

8. a way of pronouncing a word ☐ _____

9. you need money to do this ☐ _____

10. mid-day meal _____ ☐ _____

11. you sleep on this __ ☐ _____

12. What might you say about things that seem close by?

   "Hey, those things _____ near!"

▶ **Use the code to write Spelling Words.**

1	2	3	4	5	6	7	8	9	10	11	12	13
A	B	C	D	E	F	G	H	I	J	K	L	M

14	15	16	17	18	19	20	21	22	23	24	25	26
N	O	P	Q	R	S	T	U	V	W	X	Y	Z

13. <u>19 15 3 3 5 18</u> _____

14. <u>8 15 12 12 15 23</u> _____

15. <u>3 12 1 19 19 9 3</u> _____

16. <u>3 15 12 12 5 7 5</u> _____

17. <u>19 5 18 22 9 3 5</u> _____

18. <u>10 5 18 19 5 25</u> _____

19. <u>19 21 2 10 5 3 20</u> _____

20. <u>3 15 13 16 12 5 20 5</u> _____

Spelling Words

1. castle
2. handle
3. ruffle
4. icicle
5. fable
6. soccer
7. appear
8. hollow
9. classic
10. college
11. accent
12. service
13. jersey
14. mother
15. problem
16. subject
17. complete
18. mattress
19. purchase
20. luncheon

Spelling Practice Book
© Harcourt • Grade 4

Name _____

▶ **Rearrange the syllables to write Spelling Words.**

soc hol cer low

1. _____

2. _____

sic pear ap clas

3. _____

4. _____

lege cent ac col

5. _____

6. _____

1. castle
2. handle
3. ruffle
4. icicle
5. fable
6. soccer
7. appear
8. hollow
9. classic
10. college
11. accent
12. service
13. jersey
14. mother
15. problem
16. subject
17. complete
18. mattress
19. purchase
20. luncheon

▶ **Write the Spelling Word that best completes each analogy.**

7. *Clothing* is to *shirt* as *meal* is to _____.

8. *Uncle* is to *aunt* as *father* is to _____.

9. *Paint* is to *brush* as _____ is to *money*.

10. *Boil* is to *steam* as *freeze* is to _____.

11. *Cushion* is to *sofa* as _____ is to *bed*.

12. *Science* is to *experiment* as *math* is to _____.

13. *Begin* is to *finish* as *start* is to _____.

14. *Sing* is to *song* as *tell* is to _____.

▶ **Unscramble the letters to write a Spelling Word.**

15. cbusejt _____

16. riescve _____

17. adelhn _____

18. reesjy _____

19. lufref _____

20. eastlc _____

▶ **Write the missing vowels to complete the Spelling Words. Then write the words.**

1. pr__bl__m   _____

2. j__rs__y   _____

3. s__bj__ct   _____

4. m__th__r   _____

5. s__rv__c__   _____

▶ **Write the Spelling Word that is the opposite of each word.**

6. sell   _____

7. vanish   _____

8. solid   _____

9. partial   _____

10. shack   _____

11. smooth   _____

12. kindergarten   _____

▶ **Write the Spelling Word to complete each list.**

13. pot, top, _____

14. language, sound, _____

15. meal, midday, _____   18. frozen, stick, _____

16. story, lesson, _____   19. old, important, _____

17. sheets, bed, _____   20. sport, kick, _____

Spelling Words

1. castle
2. handle
3. ruffle
4. icicle
5. fable
6. soccer
7. appear
8. hollow
9. classic
10. college
11. accent
12. service
13. jersey
14. mother
15. problem
16. subject
17. complete
18. mattress
19. purchase
20. luncheon

Name _____

► **Draw a line between the two syllables that make a Spelling Word. Then write the Spelling Word.**

1. com   a. chase   _____

2. mat   b. plete   _____

3. lunch   c. tress   _____

4. pur   d. eon   _____

► **Perform the math operation to write a Spelling Word.**

5. cold – d + leg + e =   _____

6. candle – c + h =   _____

7. brother – br + m =   _____

8. ace – e + cent =   _____

9. hold – d + low =   _____

10. table – t + f =   _____

11. spear – s + ap =   _____

12. serve – e + ice =   _____

13. classy – y + ic =   _____

14. crash – r – h + tle =   _____

Spelling Words

1. castle
2. handle
3. ruffle
4. icicle
5. fable
6. soccer
7. appear
8. hollow
9. classic
10. college
11. accent
12. service
13. jersey
14. mother
15. problem
16. subject
17. complete
18. mattress
19. purchase
20. luncheon

► **Write a Spelling Word that matches each clue.**

15. dress trim   _____

16. frozen water   _____

17. sport   _____

18. something to wear   _____

19. difficulty   _____

20. part of a sentence   _____

Name _____

▶ **Fold the paper along the dotted line. As each Spelling Word is read aloud, write it in the blank. Then unfold your paper and check your work. Practice writing any Spelling Words you missed.**

1. _____

2. _____

3. _____

4. _____

5. _____

6. _____

7. _____

8. _____

9. _____

10. _____

11. _____

12. _____

13. _____

14. _____

15. _____

16. _____

17. _____

18. _____

19. _____

20. _____

Spelling Words

1. begin
2. vanish
3. bonus
4. legal
5. event
6. moment
7. motive
8. native
9. suburb
10. mimic
11. paper
12. pilot
13. raven
14. rival
15. relish
16. silent
17. solar
18. spider
19. super
20. virus

School–Home Connection

Think of a word or phrase that means the same as each Spelling Word. Have your child write the matching Spelling Word on a sheet of paper.

43

Spelling Practice Book
© Harcourt • Grade 4

Name _____

▶ **Write a Spelling Word to replace each underlined word.**

We live in a **(1)** town near a large city. We often eat outside in order to enjoy the **(2)** sun's rays. One **(3)** quiet morning, I felt something **(4)** start to move near my foot. It was a green anole, a small lizard. Green anoles are **(5)** from that area to the South. They change colors to **(6)** imitate their surroundings. This helps them **(7)** disappear the **(8)** minute they are spotted. The chameleon is a **(9)** terrific creature to have around. It is an **(10)** occasion when we find one.

1. _____   6. _____

2. _____   7. _____

3. _____   8. _____

4. _____   9. _____

5. _____   10. _____

Spelling Words

1. begin
2. vanish
3. bonus
4. legal
5. event
6. moment
7. motive
8. native
9. suburb
10. mimic
11. paper
12. pilot
13. raven
14. rival
15. relish
16. silent
17. solar
18. spider
19. super
20. virus

▶ **Write a Spelling Word to complete each list.**

11. lawful, official, _____

12. pen, pencil, _____

13. crow, black, _____

14. web, insect, _____

15. mustard, hotdog, _____

16. germ, bacteria, _____

▶ **Write the following Spelling Words:** *bonus, motive, pilot,* **and** *rival.* **Use your best handwriting.**

17. _____   19. _____

18. _____   20. _____

Handwriting Tip

Be sure that all your letters sit on the bottom line.

value

44

Name _____

▶ Write the Spelling Word that is similar to each word in the list.

1. blackbird _____

2. permitted _____

3. copy _____

4. quiet _____

5. illness _____

6. reason _____

7. extra _____

8. fantastic _____

9. challenger _____

10. happening _____

Spelling Words

1. begin
2. vanish
3. bonus
4. legal
5. event
6. moment
7. motive
8. native
9. suburb
10. mimic
11. paper
12. pilot
13. raven
14. rival
15. relish
16. silent
17. solar
18. spider
19. super
20. virus

▶ Write these Spelling Words in alphabetical order.

| solar | native | suburb |
| relish | spider | |

11. _____

12. _____

13. _____

14. _____

15. _____

 Spelling Strategy

Sounds and Letters: When you try to spell a word, say it to yourself. Picture the way the word is spelled.

Spelling Practice Book
© Harcourt • Grade 4

Name _____

▶ **RHYMING RIDDLES: Answer each riddle with a Spelling Word.**

1. What do you call an eight-legged creature that takes up too much room? A wider _____

2. What do we say when we ask to borrow someone's prize money? Loan us your _____.

3. What do you call a bird that knows the law? A _____ eagle

4. What does someone who makes noise in a neighborhood do? Disturb the _____

5. What do you call someone who likes to walk in the sunshine? A _____ stroller

▶ **ANALOGIES: Write the Spelling Word that best completes each analogy.**

6. *Show up* is to *appear* as *go away* is to _____.

7. *Conclude* is to *end* as *launch* is to _____.

8. *Wheat* is to *flour* as *wood* is to _____.

9. *Ship* is to *captain* as *airplane* is to _____.

10. *Second* is to *instant* as *minute* is to _____.

▶ **WORD SCRAMBLE: Unscramble the letters to write a Spelling Word.**

11. vitane _____   14. rsviu _____

12. stienl _____   15. lavir _____

13. vneet _____

Spelling Words

1. begin
2. vanish
3. bonus
4. legal
5. event
6. moment
7. motive
8. native
9. suburb
10. mimic
11. paper
12. pilot
13. raven
14. rival
15. relish
16. silent
17. solar
18. spider
19. super
20. virus

Name _____

▶ Fold the paper along the dotted line. As each Spelling Word is read aloud, write it in the blank. Then unfold your paper and check your work. Practice writing any Spelling Words you missed.

1. _____
2. _____
3. _____
4. _____
5. _____
6. _____
7. _____
8. _____
9. _____
10. _____
11. _____
12. _____
13. _____
14. _____
15. _____
16. _____
17. _____
18. _____
19. _____
20. _____

Spelling Words

1. reuse
2. restart
3. retell
4. resend
5. replace
6. uncork
7. unstuck
8. unannounced
9. unpleasant
10. unchain
11. unfit
12. nonprofit
13. nonmetal
14. recall
15. nontoxic
16. unwelcome
17. reproduce
18. retrace
19. uninvited
20. reapply

School–Home Connection

On a sheet of paper, make three columns. At the top of each column, write the prefix (*re-, un-, non-*). Have your child write the Spelling Words that belong in each column.

47

Name _____

▶ **Write the Spelling Word that best fits each clue.**

1. pried loose _____

2. begin again _____

3. copy _____

4. not poison _____

5. without calling _____

6. remember _____

7. unhook _____

8. write over _____

9. not wanted _____

10. mail again _____

1. reuse
2. restart
3. retell
4. resend
5. replace
6. uncork
7. unstuck
8. unannounced
9. unpleasant
10. unchain
11. unfit
12. nonprofit
13. nonmetal
14. recall
15. nontoxic
16. unwelcome
17. reproduce
18. retrace
19. uninvited
20. reapply

▶ **Read each base word. Then circle the correct prefix. Add the prefix to write a Spelling Word.**

11. cork   un-   non- _____

12. metal   un-   non- _____

13. pleasant   un-   non- _____

14. invited   un-   non- _____

15. profit   un-   non- _____

16. fit   un-   non- _____

▶ **Write the following Spelling Words: *reuse, retell, replace,* and *reapply*. Use your best handwriting.**

17. _____   19. _____

18. _____   20. _____

Handwriting Tip

When you write the letter *r*, make sure to curve up and then down twice.

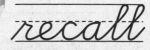

recall

48

Spelling Practice Book
© Harcourt • Grade 4

Name _____

▶ **Read each word group below. Then write the Spelling Word that belongs in each group.**

1. useful, useless, _____

2. resume, start over, _____

3. explain, tell again, _____

4. forward, repeat, _____

5. change, renew, _____

6. remember, remind, _____

7. copy, remake, _____

8. mark, go back, _____

9. application, applied, _____

Spelling Words

1. reuse
2. restart
3. retell
4. resend
5. replace
6. uncork
7. unstuck
8. unannounced
9. unpleasant
10. unchain
11. unfit
12. nonprofit
13. nonmetal
14. recall
15. nontoxic
16. unwelcome
17. reproduce
18. retrace
19. uninvited
20. reapply

▶ **Write a Spelling Word to complete each sentence.**

10. The eruption was a terrifying, _____ event.

11. The heat and magma seemed to _____ the top of the volcano.

12. Because of the ash, the area around the volcano is _____ for living things.

13. There are few areas where the ground is _____.

14. The Red Cross is a _____ group which helps disaster victims.

🔤 Spelling Strategy

Base Words: When you are writing a word with a prefix, identify the base word. Then think about the meaning of each word part. Use a dictionary to check the word's meaning.

Spelling Practice Book
© Harcourt • Grade 4

Name _____

► Complete the crossword puzzle with Spelling Words.
  Use the clues to help you.

1. reuse
2. restart
3. retell
4. resend
5. replace
6. uncork
7. unstuck
8. unannounced
9. unpleasant
10. unchain
11. unfit
12. nonprofit
13. nonmetal
14. recall
15. nontoxic
16. unwelcome
17. reproduce
18. retrace
19. uninvited
20. reapply

ACROSS
2. remove stopper
5. not nice
8. put back
9. use again
10. write over

DOWN
1. not proper
3. make again
4. begin again
6. not made of metal
7. sign up again

► Complete each sentence with a Spelling Word.

11. The mosquitoes in our campsite were _____ guests.

12. The letter came back, so I'll have to _____ it.

13. We had to _____ the fence so we could get in.

14. The paper became _____ after Amy pulled it free.

15. The audience was surprised when the singer

    came on stage _____.

Name _____

▶ Fold the paper along the dotted line. As each Spelling Word is read aloud, write it in the blank. Then unfold your paper and check your work. Practice writing any Spelling Words you missed.

1. _____
2. _____
3. _____
4. _____
5. _____
6. _____
7. _____
8. _____
9. _____
10. _____
11. _____
12. _____
13. _____
14. _____
15. _____
16. _____
17. _____
18. _____
19. _____
20. _____

Spelling Words

1. likable
2. removable
3. printable
4. adorable
5. comfortable
6. durable
7. usable
8. invisible
9. responsible
10. darkness
11. tidiness
12. silliness
13. excitement
14. government
15. requirement
16. loneliness
17. harmless
18. hopeless
19. fearless
20. horrible

School–Home Connection

Think of a word or phrase that means the opposite of each Spelling Word. Have your child say and spell the matching Spelling Word. Review any words that were missed.

Spelling Practice Book

Name _____

▶ **Write the base word of each Spelling Word.**

1. likable   _____

2. removable   _____

3. printable   _____

4. adorable   _____

5. comfortable   _____

6. usable   _____

7. excitement   _____

8. government   _____

9. requirement   _____

10. harmless   _____

11. hopeless   _____

12. fearless   _____

13. horrible   _____

14. responsible   _____

▶ **Write the following Spelling Words:** *darkness, tidiness, silliness, durable, invisible,* **and** *loneliness.* **Use your best handwriting.**

15. _____   18. _____

16. _____   19. _____

17. _____   20. _____

Spelling Words

1. likable
2. removable
3. printable
4. adorable
5. comfortable
6. durable
7. usable
8. invisible
9. responsible
10. darkness
11. tidiness
12. silliness
13. excitement
14. government
15. requirement
16. loneliness
17. harmless
18. hopeless
19. fearless
20. horrible

Handwriting Tip

Be sure to use only one stroke when joining another letter to the letter *n*.

_____

print

52

Name _____

▶ **Write a Spelling Word to replace each underlined word.**

Even in the **(1)** dimness created by the cloud of smoke, Jamie was **(2)** not afraid. With the sirens blaring, he could feel his **(3)** eagerness build. As a firefighter, he was always **(4)** reliable and ready to help. **(5)** At ease in his **(6)** sturdy boots and turnout gear, he quickly surveyed the scene.

"I'm going in," he said. Soon he was **(7)** unseen, surrounded by smoke and flames. Bravery is a **(8)** necessary thing for firefighters, and Jamie was certainly brave.

1. _____   5. _____

2. _____   6. _____

3. _____   7. _____

4. _____   8. _____

▶ **Write the Spelling Word that matches each mini-definition.**

9. being neat _____

10. can be printed _____

11. pleasant or easy to like _____

12. runs a nation, state, or city _____

13. foolish or not serious _____

14. cute _____

15. will come off _____

Spelling Words

1. likable
2. removable
3. printable
4. adorable
5. comfortable
6. durable
7. usable
8. invisible
9. responsible
10. darkness
11. tidiness
12. silliness
13. excitement
14. government
15. requirement
16. loneliness
17. harmless
18. hopeless
19. fearless
20. horrible

Spelling Strategy

Word Parts: When adding a suffix, you may need to change the spelling of the base word. For example, in the word *lonely* you change the *y* to *i* before adding the ending *-ness*.

Spelling Practice Book
© Harcourt • Grade 4

Name _____

▶ **WHAT AM I?:** Write the Spelling Word that describes each phrase.

1. baby rabbit _____

2. mayor's office _____

3. must have this _____

4. feeling sad _____

5. skydiver's feeling _____

Spelling Words

1. likable
2. removable
3. printable
4. adorable
5. comfortable
6. durable
7. usable
8. invisible
9. responsible
10. darkness
11. tidiness
12. silliness
13. excitement
14. government
15. requirement
16. loneliness
17. harmless
18. hopeless
19. fearless
20. horrible

▶ **BREAK THE CODE:** Use the code below to write Spelling Words.

1	2	3	4	5	6	7	8	9	10	11	12	13
A	B	C	D	E	F	G	H	I	J	K	L	M

14	15	16	17	18	19	20	21	22	23	24	25	26
N	O	P	Q	R	S	T	U	V	W	X	Y	Z

6. 21 19 1 2 12 5 _____

7. 18 5 13 15 22 1 2 12 5 _____

8. 8 15 18 18 9 2 12 5 _____

9. 5 24 3 9 20 5 13 5 14 20 _____

10. 12 15 14 5 12 9 14 5 19 19 _____

▶ **WORD OPERATIONS:** Perform the math operation to write a Spelling Word.

11. like – e + able _____

12. tidy – y + i + ness _____

13. response – e + ible _____

14. silly – y + i + ness _____

15. adore – e + able _____

54

Name _____

▶ Fold the paper along the dotted line. As each Spelling Word is read aloud, write it in the blank. Then unfold your paper and check your work. Practice writing any Spelling Words you missed.

1. _____
2. _____
3. _____
4. _____
5. _____
6. _____
7. _____
8. _____
9. _____
10. _____
11. _____
12. _____
13. _____
14. _____
15. _____
16. _____
17. _____
18. _____
19. _____
20. _____

Spelling Words

1. apron
2. button
3. canyon
4. certain
5. chicken
6. cardigan
7. cotton
8. dragon
9. even
10. fountain
11. gallon
12. horizon
13. listen
14. orphan
15. pardon
16. pollen
17. prison
18. siren
19. swollen
20. driven

School–Home Connection

Have your child write and cut out the Spelling Words and sort them according to their endings: -on, -ain, -en, and -an.

55

► **Write a Spelling Word to complete each list.**

1. talk, hear, _____

2. duck, turkey, _____

3. pint, quart, _____

4. silk, wool, _____

5. whistle, alarm, _____

6. water, drink, _____

7. flat, straight, _____

8. zipper, fasten, _____

9. cover, smock, _____

10. hill, valley, _____

Spelling Words

1. apron
2. button
3. canyon
4. certain
5. chicken
6. cardigan
7. cotton
8. dragon
9. even
10. fountain
11. gallon
12. horizon
13. listen
14. orphan
15. pardon
16. pollen
17. prison
18. siren
19. swollen
20. driven

► **Write a Spelling Word to complete each sentence.**

11. The sun sets over the _____.

12. Spring rains make rivers and streams _____.

13. In summer the flowers give off _____, which makes some of us sneeze.

14. Winter is _____ to bring cold days.

15. My sister has never _____ in a blizzard.

16. On summer nights, you might only need a _____ to stay warm.

► **Write the following Spelling Words:** *dragon, orphan, pardon,* and *prison.* **Use your best handwriting.**

17. _____   19. _____

18. _____   20. _____

Handwriting Tip

When you write the letter combination *on*, be sure to keep the joining stroke off the bottom line.

_____
on

Name _____

▶ **Write the Spelling Word that is the opposite of each word.**

1. lopsided   _____

2. mountain   _____

3. shrunken   _____

4. unsure   _____

5. talk   _____

▶ **Write the Spelling Word that completes each item.**

6. _____ your jacket.

7. That _____ flew the coop.

8. the police _____

9. I beg your _____.

10. a fire-breathing _____

▶ **Write these Spelling Words in alphabetical order.**

| pollen   driven   cardigan |
| prison   horizon |

11. _____

12. _____

13. _____

14. _____

15. _____

Spelling Words

1. apron
2. button
3. canyon
4. certain
5. chicken
6. cardigan
7. cotton
8. dragon
9. even
10. fountain
11. gallon
12. horizon
13. listen
14. orphan
15. pardon
16. pollen
17. prison
18. siren
19. swollen
20. driven

Spelling Strategy

Comparing Spellings: When you are unsure of the spelling of a word that ends with the sound /ən/, write it using different spellings and choose the one that looks correct. Then check your spelling in a dictionary.

Spelling Practice Book
© Harcourt • Grade 4

► **MIX AND MATCH:** Rearrange the four syllables to write two Spelling Words.

a par pron don   1. _____

    2. _____

phan or on drag   3. _____

    4. _____

yon en can chick   5. _____

    6. _____

ren en driv si   7. _____

    8. _____

► **WORD SORT:** Read the chart headings. Then write the Spelling Words where they belong.

Words with Double *l*	Words That End in *-ain*
9. _____	14. _____
10. _____	15. _____
11. _____	

Words with Double *t*	
12. _____	
13. _____	

Spelling Words

1. apron
2. button
3. canyon
4. certain
5. chicken
6. cardigan
7. cotton
8. dragon
9. even
10. fountain
11. gallon
12. horizon
13. listen
14. orphan
15. pardon
16. pollen
17. prison
18. siren
19. swollen
20. driven

Name _____

▶ **Unscramble the letters to write a Spelling Word.**

1. lrvia _____   3. eevtn _____

2. oemnmt _____   4. aslro _____

▶ **Write the Spelling Word that is similar to each clue.**

5. go over again _____

6. a type of cloth _____

7. unafraid _____

8. spray of water _____

9. pay attention _____

10. recycle _____

▶ **Perform the math operation to write a Spelling Word.**

11. more – m – e + phan = _____

12. like – e + able = _____

13. come – e + ſort + able = _____

14. un + announce – e + ed = _____

15. un + please – e + ant = _____

16. non + metal = _____

17. in + visit – t + ble = _____

18. squirrel – s + re – rel + ement = _____

19. horror – or + ible = _____

20. lonely – y + i + ness = _____

Spelling Words

1. event
2. rival
3. solar
4. moment
5. unannounced
6. reuse
7. retrace
8. unpleasant
9. nonmetal
10. likable
11. comfortable
12. horrible
13. invisible
14. loneliness
15. requirement
16. fearless
17. cotton
18. listen
19. fountain
20. orphan

Spelling Practice Book
© Harcourt • Grade 4

Name _____

▶ Unscramble the syllables to write Spelling Words with the prefixes *re-, un-, non-*.

1. nounce an un ed _____

2. al non met _____

3. trace re _____

4. use re _____

5. pleas un ant _____

▶ Change one or two letters in each word to write a Spelling Word.

6. button _____   9. color _____

7. listed _____   10. royal _____

8. mountain _____   11. nearness _____

▶ Use Spelling Words to solve the puzzle.

Spelling Words

1. event
2. rival
3. solar
4. moment
5. unannounced
6. reuse
7. retrace
8. unpleasant
9. nonmetal
10. likable
11. comfortable
12. horrible
13. invisible
14. loneliness
15. requirement
16. fearless
17. cotton
18. listen
19. fountain
20. orphan

ACROSS
14. Sadness from being alone
16. Without parents
18. An occasion
19. Something necessary
20. Nice or pleasant

DOWN
12. Relaxed or cozy
13. One _____, please
15. Can't be seen
17. Awful

60

Name _____

► **Unscramble the syllables to write Spelling Words.**

1. li ness lone   loneliness

2. a fort ble com   _____

3. ble vis in i   _____

4. ment re quire   _____

5. less fear   fearless

6. ri hor ble   _____

7. ble a lik   _____

► **Write the Spelling Word that best completes each analogy.**

8. *Friend* is to *enemy* as *partner* is to _____.

9. *Sheep* is to *wool* as *plant* is to _____.

10. *Sun* is to *moon* as _____ is to *lunar.*

11. *Look* is to *see* as *hear* is to _____.

12. *Volcano* is to *lava* as _____ is to *water.*

► **Find and circle eight Spelling Words in the puzzle. Then write the words on the lines below.**

u	n	a	n	n	o	u	n	c	e	d	a	e	n
r	e	k	b	g	a	e	y	r	b	m	r	v	d
p	u	n	p	l	e	a	s	a	n	t	e	e	x
h	n	o	r	p	h	a	n	s	h	o	u	n	t
a	n	r	e	t	r	a	c	e	r	r	s	t	j
n	o	n	m	e	t	a	l	m	o	m	e	n	t

13. _____   17. _____

14. _____   18. _____

15. _____   19. _____

16. _____   20. _____

Spelling Words

1. event
2. rival
3. solar
4. moment
5. unannounced
6. reuse
7. retrace
8. unpleasant
9. nonmetal
10. likable
11. comfortable
12. horrible
13. invisible
14. loneliness
15. requirement
16. fearless
17. cotton
18. listen
19. fountain
20. orphan

Name _____

▶ **Write the missing vowels to complete the Spelling Words. Then write the words.**

1. c__tt__n _____

2. l__st__n _____

3. __rph__n _____

▶ **Write the Spelling Word that fits each clue. Then unscramble the letters in the boxes to answer the riddle.**

4. You get water from a ___ [ ] _____

5. opponent [ ] _____

6. from the sun [ ] _____

7. a brief period of time ___ [ ] ___

8. terrible _____ [ ]

9. What is a recycler's motto? "Choose to _____!"

▶ **Write a Spelling Word to complete each word group.**

10. eventually, eventful, _____

11. vision, visibility, _____

12. comfort, discomfort, _____

13. trace, tracing, _____

14. fear, fearful, _____

15. require, requiring, _____

16. alone, lonely, _____

17. like, dislike, _____

18. metal, metallic, _____

19. pleasant, pleasantly, _____

20. announce, announcer, _____

Spelling Words

1. event
2. rival
3. solar
4. moment
5. unannounced
6. reuse
7. retrace
8. unpleasant
9. nonmetal
10. likable
11. comfortable
12. horrible
13. invisible
14. loneliness
15. requirement
16. fearless
17. cotton
18. listen
19. fountain
20. orphan

62

► Fold the paper along the dotted line. As each Spelling Word is read aloud, write it in the blank. Then unfold your paper and check your work. Practice writing any Spelling Words you missed.

1. _____
2. _____
3. _____
4. _____
5. _____
6. _____
7. _____
8. _____
9. _____
10. _____
11. _____
12. _____
13. _____
14. _____
15. _____
16. _____
17. _____
18. _____
19. _____
20. _____

Spelling Words

1. tropical
2. animal
3. April
4. arrival
5. trample
6. bottle
7. camel
8. capital
9. couple
10. swivel
11. festival
12. gentle
13. level
14. national
15. normal
16. tremble
17. puddle
18. rebel
19. single
20. tunnel

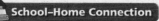
School–Home Connection

Read aloud each Spelling Word. Have your child spell each word. Then, list several words that rhyme with each one.

63

Name _____

▶ **Write a Spelling Word to replace the underlined words.**

I have entered a (1) <u>countrywide</u> Invention Fair. My entry will be judged by scientists from our nation's (2) <u>center of government</u>. I sent the (3) <u>one</u> idea that I liked best: The Garden Protector. It keeps (4) <u>any</u> creature from ruining our (5) <u>tropic-like</u> garden. My dog likes to (6) <u>walk</u> on Mom's flowers. Once Fluffy even dug a (7) <u>passageway</u> under the fence! The Garden Protector will (8) <u>shake</u> and send out a sound whenever an animal comes near.

1. _____   5. _____

2. _____   6. _____

3. _____   7. _____

4. _____   8. _____

▶ **Write a Spelling Word to complete each list.**

9. February, March, _____

10. jar, can, _____

11. two, pair, _____

12. fair, celebration, _____

13. calm, mild, _____

14. usual, regular, _____

15. even, flat, _____

16. pool, pond, _____

▶ **Write the following Spelling Words:** *swivel, arrival, camel,* **and** *rebel.* **Use your best handwriting.**

17. _____   19. _____

18. _____   20. _____

Spelling Words

1. tropical
2. animal
3. April
4. arrival
5. trample
6. bottle
7. camel
8. capital
9. couple
10. swivel
11. festival
12. gentle
13. level
14. national
15. normal
16. tremble
17. puddle
18. rebel
19. single
20. tunnel

Handwriting Tip

When you write the letter *l*, make sure it touches both the top and bottom lines.

64

Name _____

▶ **Fill in the missing letters to complete each Spelling Word. Then write each word.**

1. tramp _L_ _e_   _trample_
2. bott _L_ _e_   _bottle_
3. anim _a_ _l_   _Animal_
4. tunn _e_ _l_   _tunnal_
5. coup _L_ _e_   _Couple_
6. sing _l_ _e_   _Single_
7. lev _ _ _ _   _____
8. swiv _ _ _ _   _____
9. arriv _ _ _ _   _____
10. reb _ _ _ _   _____
11. norm _ _ _ _   _____
12. festiv _ _ _ _   _____

▶ **Unscramble the syllables to write two Spelling Words.**

A trop i pril cal   13. _____

   14. _____

el cap cam i tal   15. _____

   16. _____

tle al gen tion na   17. _____

   18. _____

Spelling Words

1. tropical
2. ~~animal~~
3. April
4. arrival
5. ~~trample~~
6. ~~bottle~~
7. ~~camel~~
8. capital
9. ~~couple~~
10. swivel
11. festival
12. gentle
13. level
14. national
15. normal
16. tremble
17. puddle
18. rebel
19. ~~single~~
20. ~~tunnel~~

▶ **Spelling Strategy**

Comparing Spellings: When you find a word that looks misspelled, try writing it another way. Use a dictionary to see which spelling is correct.

Spelling Practice Book
© Harcourt • Grade 4

► **SOLVE THE PUZZLE:** Use the clues to help you choose
Spelling Words that will solve the
puzzle. Write answers in the puzzle.

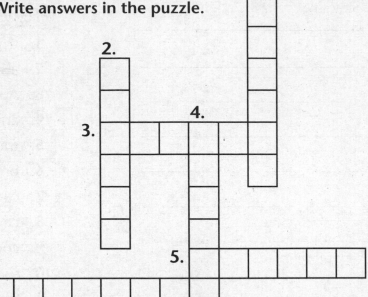

Spelling Words

1. tropical
2. animal
3. April
4. arrival
5. trample
6. bottle
7. camel
8. capital
9. couple
10. swivel
11. festival
12. gentle
13. level
14. national
15. normal
16. tremble
17. puddle
18. rebel
19. single
20. tunnel

ACROSS

3. Dig a _____

5. _____, vegetable,
   or mineral

6. A carnival

DOWN

1. A _____ touch

2. _____ opener

4. Typical or ordinary

► **WORD OPERATIONS:** Perform the math
operation to write a Spelling Word.

7. name – me + tion + al   _____

8. Ape – e + ril   _____

9. trampoline – oline + le   _____

10. cousin – sin + ple   _____

11. l + even – n + l   _____

12. arrive – e + al   _____

13. animate – te + l   _____

14. singer – er + le   _____

15. tropics – s + al   _____

66

Spelling Practice Book
© Harcourt • Grade 4

Name _____

▶ **Fold the paper along the dotted line. As each Spelling Word is read aloud, write it in the blank. Then unfold your paper and check your work. Practice writing any Spelling Words you missed.**

1. _____
2. _____
3. _____
4. _____
5. _____
6. _____
7. _____
8. _____
9. _____
10. _____
11. _____
12. _____
13. _____
14. _____
15. _____
16. _____
17. _____
18. _____
19. _____
20. _____

Spelling Words

1. lunar
2. cellar
3. collar
4. corner
5. danger
6. director
7. doctor
8. dollar
9. tinker
10. finger
11. honor
12. horror
13. labor
14. master
15. motor
16. ancestor
17. checkers
18. power
19. regular
20. sugar

School–Home Connection

Have your child write the Spelling Words on a sheet of paper. Then, have your child cut out the words and arrange them in alphabetical order.

67

Name _____

► **Write a Spelling Word to complete each sentence.**

1. Emily is a _____ at making art.

2. She likes to _____ with paints and clay.

3. Sometimes she even uses _____ paints.

4. One of her paintings shows the moon in a lovely

   _____ scene.

5. Emily painted a _____ helping a patient.

6. Emily's favorite _____ was also an artist.

7. Emily's grandmother wore a dress with a lace

   _____.

8. It is an _____ to have artistic talents.

► **Write a Spelling Word that is similar to each word in the list.**

9. work _____

10. basement _____

11. engine _____

12. board game _____

13. angle _____

14. sweetener _____

15. money _____

16. hazard _____

► **Write the following Spelling Words:** *director, horror, power,* **and** *regular.* **Use your best handwriting.**

17. _____   19. _____

18. _____   20. _____

Spelling Words

1. lunar
2. cellar
3. collar
4. corner
5. danger
6. director
7. doctor
8. dollar
9. tinker
10. finger
11. honor
12. horror
13. labor
14. master
15. motor
16. ancestor
17. checkers
18. power
19. regular
20. sugar

Handwriting Tip

Be careful when you connect the vowels *a, o,* and *e* to *r,* or the *r* could look like an *i.*

_____

or, er

Name _____

▶ Write the Spelling Word that best completes each phrase.

1. turn the _____

2. spend a _dollar_____

3. a _____ eclipse

4. a cold, underground _____

5. _____ tools

6. please pass the _sugar_____

7. call the _doctor_____

8. the dog's _____

▶ Write a Spelling Word that goes with each clue.

9. leader of the actors in a movie _____

10. relative who lived very long ago _____

11. part of the hand; not the thumb _____

▶ Write these Spelling Words in alphabetical order.

horror	motor	honor	checkers

12. _____

13. _____

14. _____

15. _____

🔤 **Spelling Strategy**

Guessing and Checking: If you are not sure how to spell a word that ends with the /ər/ sound, make a guess. Then check a dictionary to see if you are right.

Spelling Practice Book
© Harcourt • Grade 4

Name _____

▶ **RHYMING RIDDLES: Create a rhyming answer for each riddle using a Spelling Word.**

1. What do you do when you help the person next door?

   _____ for your neighbor

2. What do you call a boat that sails under a full moon?

   A _____ schooner

▶ **WORD SCRAMBLE: Unscramble the letters to write a Spelling Word.**

3. gfiner   _____

4. grlraeu   _____

5. trocod   _____

▶ **WORD SEARCH: Find and circle ten Spelling Words. Then write the words on the lines below.**

y	p	k	d	o	l	l	a	r	h	t	l
p	o	m	a	s	t	e	r	b	o	i	r
a	w	a	n	c	e	s	t	o	r	n	h
h	e	b	g	t	s	u	g	a	r	k	u
a	r	c	e	l	l	a	r	m	o	e	v
r	u	p	r	n	m	o	t	o	r	r	i

6. _____   11. _____

7. _____   12. _____

8. _____   13. _____

9. _____   14. _____

10. _____   15. _____

Spelling Words

1. lunar
2. cellar
3. collar
4. corner
5. danger
6. director
7. doctor
8. dollar
9. tinker
10. finger
11. honor
12. horror
13. labor
14. master
15. motor
16. ancestor
17. checkers
18. power
19. regular
20. sugar

Name _____

▶ Fold the paper along the dotted line. As each Spelling Word is read aloud, write it in the blank. Then unfold your paper and check your work. Practice writing any Spelling Words you missed.

1. _____

2. _____

3. _____

4. _____

5. _____

6. _____

7. _____

8. _____

9. _____

10. _____

11. _____

12. _____

13. _____

14. _____

15. _____

16. _____

17. _____

18. _____

19. _____

20. _____

Spelling Words

1. overactive
2. overbite
3. overboard
4. overdrive
5. overestimate
6. overhand
7. overheat
8. overpass
9. overreact
10. underline
11. underbrush
12. underdeveloped
13. undergo
14. underhand
15. underpass
16. underscore
17. underwater
18. submarine
19. subway
20. overact

School–Home Connection

Work with your child to write down words that begin with the word parts *over-*, *under-*, and *sub-*. Discuss the spelling and meaning of each word.

71

Spelling Practice Book
© Harcourt • Grade 4

▶ **Write the Spelling Word that fits each clue.**

1. off the side of a boat _____

2. endure a procedure _____

3. high gear _____

4. item below the water's surface _____

5. a naval vessel _____

6. a railroad below the ground _____

7. more active than normal _____

8. not normally developed _____

9. underline or emphasize _____

10. respond too strongly _____

11. draw a line below _____

12. plants that grow beneath larger trees _____

13. a road that goes below another road _____

14. to get too hot _____

15. make a guess that is too high _____

16. a road that goes above another road _____

Spelling Words

1. overactive
2. overbite
3. overboard
4. overdrive
5. overestimate
6. overhand
7. overheat
8. overpass
9. overreact
10. underline
11. underbrush
12. underdeveloped
13. undergo
14. underhand
15. underpass
16. underscore
17. underwater
18. submarine
19. subway
20. overact

▶ **Write the following Spelling Words:** *overbite, overhand, underhand,* **and** *overact.* **Use your best handwriting.**

17. _____   19. _____

18. _____   20. _____

Handwriting Tip

Be sure that all of your letters are the correct size.

over

Name _____

▶ **Write the Spelling Word that completes each sentence.**

1. The Navy has a new _____.

2. When your front teeth cover your lower lip, you have an

   _____.

3. A young actor will often _____.

4. When you draw a line below a word, you

   _____ it.

▶ **Write a Spelling Word to replace the underlined words in each phrase.**

5. more active than normal imagination _____

6. below the water's surface swimming _____

7. experience a change _____

8. go into high gear _____

9. take the underground train _____

▶ **Write the Spelling Word that is the opposite of each phrase.**

10. grown too much _____

11. keep too cold _____

12. still on a boat _____

13. large trees _____

14. predict too little _____

15. fair, aboveboard _____

Spelling Words

1. overactive
2. overbite
3. overboard
4. overdrive
5. overestimate
6. overhand
7. overheat
8. overpass
9. overreact
10. underline
11. underbrush
12. underdeveloped
13. undergo
14. underhand
15. underpass
16. underscore
17. underwater
18. submarine
19. subway
20. overact

Spelling Strategy

Word Parts: When you are unsure of the spelling of a two-part word, say the word aloud. Listen to the way each part sounds.

Spelling Practice Book
© Harcourt • Grade 4

Name _____

▶ **ANALOGIES: Write the Spelling Word that best completes each analogy.**

1. *Army* is to *tank* as *Navy* is to _____.

2. *Swimming* is to *backstroke* as *pitching* is to

   _____.

3. *Chair* is to *seat* as *bridge* is to _____.

4. *Snore* is to *sleep* as *shout* is to _____.

5. *Excess* is to *overload* as *boiling* is to _____.

▶ **UNSCRAMBLE THE SYLLABLES: Unscramble the syllables to write a Spelling Word.**

6. der line un   _____

7. tive o ac ver   _____

8. ver board o   _____

9. pass der un   _____

10. bite ver o   _____

▶ **BREAK THE CODE: Use the code below to write Spelling Words.**

1	2	3	4	5	6	7	8	9	10	11	12	13
A	B	C	D	E	F	G	H	I	J	K	L	M

14	15	16	17	18	19	20	21	22	23	24	25	26
N	O	P	Q	R	S	T	U	V	W	X	Y	Z

11. <u>19 21 2 23 1 25</u>   _____

12. <u>21 14 4 5 18 2 18 21 19 8</u>   _____

13. <u>15 22 5 18 4 18 9 22 5</u>   _____

14. <u>21 14 4 5 18 7 15</u>   _____

15. <u>21 14 4 5 18 19 3 15 18 5</u>   _____

Spelling Words

1. overactive
2. overbite
3. overboard
4. overdrive
5. overestimate
6. overhand
7. overheat
8. overpass
9. overreact
10. underline
11. underbrush
12. underdeveloped
13. undergo
14. underhand
15. underpass
16. underscore
17. underwater
18. submarine
19. subway
20. overact

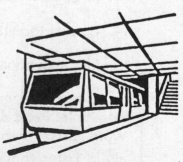

Spelling Practice Book
© Harcourt • Grade 4

Name _____

▶ Fold the paper along the dotted line. As each Spelling
Word is read aloud, write it in the blank. Then unfold
your paper and check your work. Practice writing any
Spelling Words you missed.

1. _____

2. _____

3. _____

4. _____

5. _____

6. _____

7. _____

8. _____

9. _____

10. _____

11. _____

12. _____

13. _____

14. _____

15. _____

16. _____

17. _____

18. _____

19. _____

20. _____

Spelling Words

1. babies'
2. baby's
3. child's
4. children
5. classes'
6. class's
7. sheep
8. feet
9. elk
10. fish
11. fishes'
12. goose's
13. geese
14. jeans
15. mouse's
16. mice
17. teeth
18. women
19. woman's
20. moose

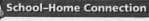

School–Home Connection

Play "Spelling Word Concentration." Have your
child write each Spelling Word on two index
cards and arrange them face down on a table.
Turn over two cards at a time to find pairs.

75

Spelling Practice Book
© Harcourt • Grade 4

Name _____

▶ **Write a Spelling Word to complete each sentence.**

Many **(1)** _____ read fables.

My **(2)** fourth-grade _____ favorite is about a

lion that spares a **(3)** small _____ life. The lion

usually ate **(4)** _____. This time the lion set

him on his **(5)** _____. Later, when the lion was

trapped, the mouse used his **(6)** _____ to free

the lion.

▶ **Write the Spelling Word that means the same as each
group of words.**

7. of more than one class _____

8. more than one adult female _____

9. more than one goose _____

10. pants made of denim _____

11. of more than one infant _____

12. belongs to a goose _____

13. belongs to a child _____

14. belongs to a female _____

15. animal with antlers _____

16. another animal with antlers _____

▶ **Write the following Spelling Words:** *fish, baby's, sheep,*
and *fishes'.* **Use your best handwriting.**

17. _____   19. _____

18. _____   20. _____

Spelling Words

1. *babies'*
2. *baby's*
3. *child's*
4. *children*
5. *classes'*
6. *class's*
7. *sheep*
8. *feet*
9. *elk*
10. *fish*
11. *fishes'*
12. *goose's*
13. *geese*
14. *jeans*
15. *mouse's*
16. *mice*
17. *teeth*
18. *women*
19. *woman's*
20. *moose*

Handwriting Tip

When you write
the letter *s,* bring
the first upstroke
to a point.
Otherwise, it
could look like
an *a.*

fish

Spelling Practice Book
© Harcourt • Grade 4

Name _____

▶ Write the Spelling Word that is the plural form of each word.

1. mouse _____

2. tooth _____

3. foot _____

4. child _____

5. sheep _____

Spelling Words

1. babies'
2. baby's
3. child's
4. children
5. classes'
6. class's
7. sheep
8. feet
9. elk
10. fish
11. fishes'
12. goose's
13. geese
14. jeans
15. mouse's
16. mice
17. teeth
18. women
19. woman's
20. moose

▶ Write a Spelling Word to complete each phrase or sentence.

6. men and _____

7. the _____ tanks

8. The _____ fly south in winter.

9. several _____ blankets

10. an order of _____ and chips

11. a new pair of _____

▶ Write the possessive form of each word.

12. baby _____

13. mouse _____

14. child _____

15. class _____

 Spelling Strategy

Using a Dictionary: If you're not sure that you spelled the plural form of a word correctly, check it in a dictionary.

Name _____

▶ **RHYMING RIDDLES: Write a Spelling Word to answer each riddle.**

1. What are eyeglasses that belong to all the students in

   the school? the _____ glasses

2. What do you call a farm animal that can jump?

   a _____ that can leap

3. What is an animal with antlers that has escaped?

   a _____ on the loose

4. What do you call frozen rodents?

   _____ on ice

▶ **CATEGORIES: Write the Spelling Words that fit in each category.**

Belonging to Animals

5. _____   7. _____

6. _____

Belonging to People

8. _____   10. _____

9. _____   11. _____

▶ **MISSING VOWELS: Write the missing vowels to complete the Spelling Words. Then write the words.**

12. t___ ___th   _____

13. j___ ___ns   _____

14. ch___ldr___n   _____

15. ___lk   _____

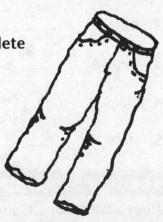

Spelling Words

1. babies'
2. baby's
3. child's
4. children
5. classes'
6. class's
7. sheep
8. feet
9. elk
10. fish
11. fishes'
12. goose's
13. geese
14. jeans
15. mouse's
16. mice
17. teeth
18. women
19. woman's
20. moose

Name _____

▶ Add *-le, -al* or *-el* to complete the Spelling Word. Then write the word on the line.

1. nation_____   _____

2. lev_____   _____

3. gent_____   _____

4. arriv_____   _____

5. sing_____   _____

▶ Change one or two letters in each word to write a Spelling Word.

6. dollar _____   9. disk _____

7. leans _____   10. woman _____

8. rowed _____   11. wreckers _____

▶ Unscramble the letters to write a Spelling Word.

12. ocdotr   _____

13. fhiss'e   _____

14. ndregou   _____

15. rdoobavre   _____

16. bawysu   _____

17. cassl's   _____

18. epshe   _____

19. rtveaeho   _____

20. uudresnhrb   _____

Spelling Words

1. arrival
2. gentle
3. national
4. single
5. level
6. collar
7. doctor
8. checkers
9. power
10. overboard
11. overheat
12. underbrush
13. undergo
14. subway
15. sheep
16. class's
17. fishes'
18. women
19. jeans
20. fish

79

Spelling Practice Book
© Harcourt • Grade 4

Name _____

▶ **Write the missing vowels to complete the Spelling Words. Then write the words.**

1. ch__ __k__ __s   _____

2. c__ ll__ r   _____

3. p__ w__ r   _____

4. d__ ct__ r   _____

▶ **Rearrange the syllables to write two Spelling Words.**

way tle gen sub

5. _____

6. _____

el wo lev men

7. _____

8. _____

le heat o sing ver

9. _____

10. _____

val un ar go ri der

11. _____

12. _____

brush un o board ver der

13. _____

14. _____

▶ **Write the Spelling Word that rhymes with each word.**

15. rational _____

16. cheap _____

17. passes _____

18. dishes _____

19. queens _____

20. wish _____

Name _____

▶ **Use the word parts in the box to write five Spelling Words.**

```
sub-      under-      over-
```

1. _____   4. _____

2. _____   5. _____

3. _____

▶ **Write a Spelling Word to complete each list.**

6. hospital, nurse, _____

7. gills, fins, _____

8. pants, denim, _____

9. animal, wool, _____

10. fishermen's, boats', _____

11. pocket, cuff, _____

12. even, flat, _____

13. triple, double, _____

14. men, children, _____

15. calm, mild, _____

16. ticket, departure, _____

17. chess, backgammon, _____

18. rule, control, _____

19. state, countrywide, _____

20. teachers', students', _____

Spelling Words

1. arrival
2. gentle
3. national
4. single
5. level
6. collar
7. doctor
8. checkers
9. power
10. overboard
11. overheat
12. underbrush
13. undergo
14. subway
15. sheep
16. class's
17. fishes'
18. women
19. jeans
20. fish

81

Name _____

▶ **Write the Spelling Word that fits each clue.**

1. farm animal that produces wool _____

2. water creatures _____

3. belonging to water creatures _____

4. denim pants _____

5. belonging to a group of students _____

6. a group of adult females _____

▶ **Write the Spelling Word that best completes each analogy.**

7. *Go* is to *stay* as *departure* is to _____.

8. *One* is to *many* as _____ is to *multiple*.

9. *Teacher* is to *student* as _____ is to *patient*.

10. *Words* are to *puzzles* as *disks* are to _____.

11. *Highway* is to *car* as _____ is to *train*.

12. *Origin* is to *original* as *nation* is to _____.

13. *Winter* is to *freeze* as *summer* is to _____.

14. *Cuff* is to *pants* as _____ is to *shirt*.

▶ **Draw a line between the two word parts that make a Spelling Word. Then write the Spelling Word.**

over	el	15. _____
go	pow	16. _____
er	under	17. _____
lev	tle	18. _____
gen	under	19. _____
brush	board	20. _____

Spelling Words

1. arrival
2. gentle
3. national
4. single
5. level
6. collar
7. doctor
8. checkers
9. power
10. overboard
11. overheat
12. underbrush
13. undergo
14. subway
15. sheep
16. class's
17. fishes'
18. women
19. jeans
20. fish

Spelling Practice Book
© Harcourt • Grade 4

Words with
Suffixes -*ant, -ent,
-eer, -ist, -ian*
Lesson 21

Name _____

▶ Fold the paper along the dotted line. As each Spelling
Word is read aloud, write it in the blank. Then unfold
your paper and check your work. Practice writing any
Spelling Words you missed.

1. _____

2. _____

3. _____

4. _____

5. _____

6. _____

7. _____

8. _____

9. _____

10. _____

11. _____

12. _____

13. _____

14. _____

15. _____

16. _____

17. _____

18. _____

19. _____

20. _____

Spelling Words

1. assistant
2. consultant
3. coolant
4. defendant
5. radiant
6. disinfectant
7. ignorant
8. absorbent
9. confident
10. different
11. engineer
12. activist
13. cyclist
14. motorist
15. pianist
16. typist
17. comedian
18. electrician
19. librarian
20. musician

School–Home Connection

Help your child cut out the Spelling Words
and sort them by suffix: -*ant, -ent, -eer, -ist,*
and -*ian.*

83

Name _____

Words with
Suffixes -ant, -ent,
-eer, -ist, -ian
Lesson 21

▶ **Read the Spelling Words. Then sort and write them where they belong.**

Words with the Suffix *-ant*	Words with the Suffix *-ent*
1. _____	8. _____
2. _____	9. _____
3. _____	10. _____
4. _____	
5. _____	
6. _____	
7. _____	

Word with the Suffix *-eer*	Words with the Suffix *-ist*
11. _____	12. _____
	13. _____
	14. _____
	15. _____
	16. _____

Spelling Words

1. assistant
2. consultant
3. coolant
4. defendant
5. radiant
6. disinfectant
7. ignorant
8. absorbent
9. confident
10. different
11. engineer
12. activist
13. cyclist
14. motorist
15. pianist
16. typist
17. comedian
18. electrician
19. librarian
20. musician

▶ **Write the following Spelling Words:** *comedian, electrician, librarian,* **and** *musician.* **Use your best handwriting.**

17. _____   19. _____

18. _____   20. _____

Handwriting Tip

Remember to use equal space between letters.

typist

Spelling Practice Book
© Harcourt • Grade 4

Name _____

Words with
Suffixes -*ant*, -*ent*,
-*eer*, -*ist*, -*ian*
Lesson 21

▶ **Write Spelling Words to complete the story.**

There are many __(1)__ people in my new town, and I
want to know them all. Mr. Hollis is a __(2)__. He rides his
bike everywhere he goes. Our __(3)__, Mrs. Lewis, helped me
find the books I needed for my report. When we needed
new lights for our house, we called Ms. Estes, an __(4)__.
She's very funny, too. I think she could be a __(5)__ on TV.
Since I've met so many people here, I feel more __(6)__ about
making new friends.

1. _____   4. _____

2. _____   5. _____

3. _____   6. _____

Spelling Words

1. assistant
2. consultant
3. coolant
4. defendant
5. radiant
6. disinfectant
7. ignorant
8. absorbent
9. confident
10. different
11. engineer
12. activist
13. cyclist
14. motorist
15. pianist
16. typist
17. comedian
18. electrician
19. librarian
20. musician

▶ **Write the Spelling Word that fits each mini-definition.**

7. someone who gives advice _____

8. a person charged with a crime _____

9. a person who plays the piano _____

10. glowing brightly _____

11. used to kill germs _____

▶ **Add a suffix to each base word to make a Spelling Word.**

12. cool   _____

13. ignore   _____

14. active   _____

15. type   _____

 Spelling Strategy

Base Words: When the base word ends in *e*, be sure to drop the final letter if the
suffix begins with a vowel. For example, with the word *cycle*, drop the *e* and add -*ist*
to make *cyclist*.

85

Name _____

Words with
Suffixes -ant, -ent,
-eer, -ist, -ian
Lesson 21

▶ **SOLVE THE PUZZLE:** Use Spelling Words to solve the puzzle.

ACROSS
2. uninformed
3. plays an instrument
8. able to soak up liquid
9. one who drives
10. uses a keyboard

DOWN
1. operates a locomotive
4. sure of one's self
5. works among books
6. helper
7. travels on two wheels

▶ **ANALOGIES:** Write the Spelling Word that best completes each analogy.

11. *Car* is to *driver* as *piano* is to _____.

12. *Dark* is to *drab* as *light* is to _____.

13. *Flour* is to *baker* as *joke* is to _____.

14. *Wood* is to *carpenter* as *wire* is to _____.

15. *Pesticide* is to *insects* as _____ is to *germs*.

Name _____

▶ Fold the paper along the dotted line. As each Spelling Word is read aloud, write it in the blank. Then unfold your paper and check your work. Practice writing any Spelling Words you missed.

1. _____

2. _____

3. _____

4. _____

5. _____

6. _____

7. _____

8. _____

9. _____

10. _____

11. _____

12. _____

13. _____

14. _____

15. _____

16. _____

17. _____

18. _____

19. _____

20. _____

Spelling Words

1. incomplete
2. indirect
3. indent
4. instead
5. include
6. inexact
7. infamous
8. outbid
9. outbreak
10. outcast
11. outdated
12. outdoor
13. downfall
14. downhill
15. downpour
16. downstairs
17. update
18. upfront
19. uphill
20. upwind

School–Home Connection

Read each Spelling Word aloud with your child. Then, have your child write the words in alphabetical order.

87

Name _____

▶ **Write a Spelling Word to complete each sentence.**

1. There was a _____ on the day we moved, so everything got wet.

2. Our new house has a basement _____.

3. We had to _____ the old appliances.

4. We will celebrate on the _____ patio.

5. Our house is _____ from a bakery.

6. I must _____ our new address on the invitations.

▶ **Write the Spelling Word that is the opposite of each word or phrase.**

7. uphill _____

8. straight _____

9. popular person _____

10. rise up _____

11. honorable _____

12. brand new _____

13. finished _____

14. specific _____

15. dishonest _____

16. downhill _____

▶ **Write the following Spelling Words:** *instead, indent, outbid,* **and** *outbreak.* **Use your best handwriting.**

17. _____   19. _____

18. _____   20. _____

Spelling Words

1. incomplete
2. indirect
3. indent
4. instead
5. include
6. inexact
7. infamous
8. outbid
9. outbreak
10. outcast
11. outdated
12. outdoor
13. downfall
14. downhill
15. downpour
16. downstairs
17. update
18. upfront
19. uphill
20. upwind

Handwriting Tip

Keep your letter strokes smooth and steady. Do not mark over strokes that you have already written.

Spelling Practice Book
© Harcourt • Grade 4

Name _____

▶ **Write a Spelling Word to replace the underlined words.**

Dear Diary,
    We just arrived in the United States, and I feel like an
(1) <u>outsider</u>. In our new home my room is **(2)** <u>below
the first floor</u>. We haven't painted yet, so my room is
(3) <u>unfinished</u>. Tomorrow, Mom will walk **(4)** <u>to the bottom
of the hill</u> with me for my first day of school. The school has
an **(5)** <u>open-air</u> eating area and a nice playground. Diary,
I will **(6)** <u>inform you</u> about my first day.

1. _____   4. _____

2. _____   5. _____

3. _____   6. _____

▶ **Write the Spelling Word that matches each clue.**

7. in place of something or someone _____

8. the way to start a paragraph _____

9. a heavy rain _____

10. a sudden eruption _____

11. to put within a group _____

▶ **Write these Spelling Words in alphabetical order.**

| upwind | upfront | outbid | uphill |

12. _____   14. _____

13. _____   15. _____

🔤 **Spelling Strategy**

Proofread with a Partner: When you write, work with a partner to check each
other's spelling.

Spelling Words

1. incomplete
2. indirect
3. indent
4. instead
5. include
6. inexact
7. infamous
8. outbid
9. outbreak
10. outcast
11. outdated
12. outdoor
13. downfall
14. downhill
15. downpour
16. downstairs
17. update
18. upfront
19. uphill
20. upwind

Spelling Practice Book
© Harcourt • Grade 4

▶ **MATCHING:** Draw a line between the two word parts that make a Spelling Word. Then write the Spelling Word.

bid	down	1. _____
down	date	2. _____
stairs	complete	3. _____
up	in	4. _____
out	out	5. _____
in	fall	6. _____
exact	break	7. _____

Spelling Words

1. incomplete
2. indirect
3. indent
4. instead
5. include
6. inexact
7. infamous
8. outbid
9. outbreak
10. outcast
11. outdated
12. outdoor
13. downfall
14. downhill
15. downpour
16. downstairs
17. update
18. upfront
19. uphill
20. upwind

▶ **WORD SEARCH:** Find and circle eight Spelling Words in the puzzle. Then write the words on the lines below.

u	o	u	t	d	a	t	e	d	n
p	i	i	i	d	b	c	z	i	v
f	n	d	n	o	u	p	l	n	o
r	f	g	d	w	p	d	z	d	u
o	a	w	i	n	w	z	a	e	t
n	m	w	r	h	i	n	w	n	d
t	o	j	e	i	n	c	b	t	o
e	u	x	c	l	d	q	s	e	o
r	s	w	t	l	l	p	w	i	r

8. _____   12. _____

9. _____   13. _____

10. _____   14. _____

11. _____   15. _____

Name _____

▶ Fold the paper along the dotted line. As each Spelling
Word is read aloud, write it in the blank. Then unfold your
paper and check your work. Practice writing any Spelling
Words you missed.

1. _____

2. _____

3. _____

4. _____

5. _____

6. _____

7. _____

8. _____

9. _____

10. _____

11. _____

12. _____

13. _____

14. _____

15. _____

16. _____

17. _____

18. _____

19. _____

20. _____

Spelling Words

1. decoration
2. abbreviation
3. admiration
4. association
5. aviation
6. civilization
7. declaration
8. addition
9. composition
10. preposition
11. abdominal
12. proposal
13. rendition
14. disposal
15. emotional
16. environmental
17. denial
18. facial
19. judicial
20. testimonial

School–Home Connection

Have your child carefully outline each
handwritten Spelling Word. Remind him or her
to pay special attention to any tall letters and
letters that fall below the line.

91

Name _____

▶ Complete each Spelling Word by adding the missing vowels. Then write each Spelling Word.

1. d__c__r__t___n _____

2. __dd__t___n _____

3. c__mp__s__t___n _____

4. d__sp__s__l _____

5. __bbr__v___t___n _____

6. __m__t___n__l _____

7. d__cl__r__t___n _____

8. __dm__r__t___n _____

▶ Write a Spelling Word to complete each list.

9. noun, verb, _____

10. club, group, _____

11. suggestion, offer, _____

12. recycle, pollution, _____

13. people, culture, _____

14. flight, airplane, _____

15. judge, jury, _____

16. stomach, middle, _____

▶ Write the following Spelling Words: *testimonial, rendition, denial,* and *facial.* Use your best handwriting.

17. _____ 19. _____

18. _____ 20. _____

Spelling Words

1. decoration
2. abbreviation
3. admiration
4. association
5. aviation
6. civilization
7. declaration
8. addition
9. composition
10. preposition
11. abdominal
12. proposal
13. rendition
14. disposal
15. emotional
16. environmental
17. denial
18. facial
19. judicial
20. testimonial

Handwriting Tip

When you write the letters *on,* be sure to keep the joining stroke high. Otherwise *on* could look like *an.*

on an

Spelling Practice Book
© Harcourt • Grade 4

Name _____

▶ **Add a suffix to each base word to write a Spelling Word.**

1. dispose _____

2. face _____

3. testimony _____

4. propose _____

▶ **Read each Spelling Word. Then sort and write the Spelling Words that belong on the chart.**

Words with the Suffix *-ition*	Words with the Suffix *-ation*
5. _____	9. _____
6. _____	10. _____
7. _____	11. _____
8. _____	12. _____
	13. _____
	14. _____
	15. _____

Spelling Strategy

Using a Dictionary: If you need help deciding whether a word is spelled correctly, look it up in a dictionary.

Spelling Practice Book
© Harcourt • Grade 4

Name _____

▶ **WORD OPERATIONS: Perform the math operation to write a Spelling Word.**

1. propose – e + al = _____

2. deny – y + ial = _____

3. testimony – y + ial = _____

4. disposition – ition + al = _____

5. render – er + ition = _____

6. abdomen – en + inal = _____

7. declare – e + ation = _____

▶ **WHAT ARE THEY? Write the Spelling Word that completes each statement.**

8. A piece of writing can be a _____.

9. 2 + 2 is an example of _____.

10. The Incas were an ancient _____.

11. A _____ is a type of skin treatment done to the face.

12. Ribbons and banners are used as _____.

13. The Wright brothers are important to the history of _____.

14. An _____ is the short way to write a word.

15. Clubs are a type of _____.

▶ **WORD SCRAMBLE: Unscramble each group of letters to write a Spelling Word.**

16. vnntlaeeiormn _____   19. nrtaodiami _____

17. opiitrepson _____   20. ciijdlua _____

18. tanlmoeio _____

Spelling Words

1. decoration
2. abbreviation
3. admiration
4. association
5. aviation
6. civilization
7. declaration
8. addition
9. composition
10. preposition
11. abdominal
12. proposal
13. rendition
14. disposal
15. emotional
16. environmental
17. denial
18. facial
19. judicial
20. testimonial

Spelling Practice Book
© Harcourt • Grade 4

▶ **Fold the paper along the dotted line. As each Spelling Word is read aloud, write it in the blank. Then unfold your paper and check your work. Practice writing any Spelling Words you missed.**

1. _____

2. _____

3. _____

4. _____

5. _____

6. _____

7. _____

8. _____

9. _____

10. _____

11. _____

12. _____

13. _____

14. _____

15. _____

16. _____

17. _____

18. _____

19. _____

20. _____

Spelling Words

1. additional
2. beautifully
3. blissfully
4. boastfully
5. carefully
6. cheerfully
7. colorfully
8. educational
9. effortlessly
10. endlessly
11. guiltlessly
12. joyfully
13. meaningfully
14. playfully
15. restfully
16. respectfully
17. childishness
18. truthfully
19. usefully
20. powerfully

School–Home Connection

Have your child write the Spelling Words on a sheet of paper. Then circle one or more smaller words he or she sees within each word.

Spelling Practice Book
© Harcourt • Grade 4

Name _____

▶ **Write the Spelling Word that best fits each clue.**

1. with caution _____

2. with honesty _____

3. more _____

4. something that teaches _____

5. done easily _____

6. with color _____

7. with a good attitude _____

8. in a bragging way _____

9. doing something without guilt _____

10. goes on forever _____

11. immature behavior _____

12. in a way that is lovely _____

▶ **Write a Spelling Word that fits each description.**

13. helpfully _____

14. honorably _____

15. happily _____

16. strongly _____

▶ **Write the following Spelling Words:** *meaningfully, blissfully, playfully,* **and** *restfully.* **Use your best handwriting.**

17. _____

18. _____

19. _____

20. _____

Spelling Words

1. additional
2. beautifully
3. blissfully
4. boastfully
5. carefully
6. cheerfully
7. colorfully
8. educational
9. effortlessly
10. endlessly
11. guiltlessly
12. joyfully
13. meaningfully
14. playfully
15. restfully
16. respectfully
17. childishness
18. truthfully
19. usefully
20. powerfully

Handwriting Tip

Be careful not to close the top of the letter *y*, or it might look like a *g*.

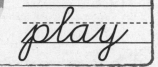

play

Spelling Practice Book
© Harcourt • Grade 4

Name _____

▶ Write a Spelling Word that is the opposite of each word
or phrase in the list.

1. with shame   _____

2. weakly   _____

3. with difficulty   _____

4. modestly   _____

5. carelessly   _____

6. dishonestly   _____

7. limited   _____

8. in a way that is ugly   _____

9. in a way that is serious   _____

▶ Read each Spelling Word. Then sort and write them
in the chart where they belong.

Words that Describe Happy Feelings	Word with the Suffix -ness
10. _____	13. _____
11. _____	**Words with the Suffix -al**
12. _____	14. _____
	15. _____

Spelling Strategy

Comparing Spellings: When you're not sure how to spell a word, try writing it in
different ways. Then, choose the spelling that looks correct.

Spelling Practice Book
© Harcourt • Grade 4

Name _____

▶ **SYLLABLE SCRAMBLE:** Unscramble the syllables to write Spelling Words.

1. ful rest ly _____

2. ly col ful or _____

3. ing ful mean ly _____

4. spect ly re ful _____

5. al ad tion di _____

6. ti ful beau ly _____

▶ **HIDDEN WORDS:** Write the Spelling Words that contain these smaller words.

7. are _____

8. lay _____

9. dish _____

10. owe _____

11. cat _____

12. fort _____

▶ **BREAK THE CODE:** Use the code below to write Spelling Words.

1	2	3	4	5	6	7	8	9	10	11	12	13
A	B	C	D	E	F	G	H	I	J	K	L	M

14	15	16	17	18	19	20	21	22	23	24	25	26
N	O	P	Q	R	S	T	U	V	W	X	Y	Z

13. <u>21</u> <u>19</u> <u>5</u> <u>6</u> <u>21</u> <u>12</u> <u>12</u> <u>25</u>   _____

14. <u>20</u> <u>18</u> <u>21</u> <u>20</u> <u>8</u> <u>6</u> <u>21</u> <u>12</u> <u>12</u> <u>25</u>   _____

15. <u>5</u> <u>14</u> <u>4</u> <u>12</u> <u>5</u> <u>19</u> <u>19</u> <u>12</u> <u>25</u>   _____

Spelling Words

1. additional
2. beautifully
3. blissfully
4. boastfully
5. carefully
6. cheerfully
7. colorfully
8. educational
9. effortlessly
10. endlessly
11. guiltlessly
12. joyfully
13. meaningfully
14. playfully
15. restfully
16. respectfully
17. childishness
18. truthfully
19. usefully
20. powerfully

Spelling Practice Book
© Harcourt • Grade 4

▶ **Write the missing vowels to complete the Spelling Words. Then write the words**

1. c__nf__d__nt _____

2. __ng__n__ __r _____

3. __l__ctr__c__ __n _____

4. r__d__ __nt _____

5. t__p__st _____

▶ **Write a Spelling Word to complete each list.**

6. exact, exactly, _____

7. emotion, unemotional, _____

8. testify, testimony, _____

9. truth, untruthful, _____

10. care, careless, _____

11. meaning, meaningless, _____

▶ **Write the Spelling Word that fits each clue.**

12. of the stomach area _____

13. in the direction the wind blows _____

14. 2 + 2 = 4 _____

15. easily _____

16. a feeling of respect or approval _____

17. honest and fair _____

18. an ornament _____

19. old-fashioned _____

20. a decline _____

99

Name _____

▶ **Unscramble the letters to write a Spelling Word.**

1. oflwandl   _____

2. trufnop   _____

3. ecxntia   _____

4. uddtoeat   _____

5. npiudw   _____

▶ **Write the Spelling Word that is the opposite of each word.**

6. dull   _____   9. disrespect _____

7. subtraction _____   10. unfeeling _____

8. unsure   _____

▶ **Find, circle, and write the ten Spelling Words that are left.**

n	c	e	n	g	i	n	e	e	r	t	w	r	e	l
r	a	b	d	o	m	i	n	a	l	r	d	u	n	y
p	r	g	t	t	r	u	t	h	f	u	l	l	y	t
a	e	c	m	e	a	n	i	n	g	f	u	l	l	y
e	f	f	o	r	t	l	e	s	s	l	y	r	o	p
b	u	t	e	s	t	i	m	o	n	i	a	l	u	i
d	l	k	t	d	e	c	o	r	a	t	i	o	n	s
q	l	l	d	d	u	o	g	x	z	b	v	a	l	t
n	y	n	e	l	e	c	t	r	i	c	i	a	n	d

11. _____   16. _____

12. _____   17. _____

13. _____   18. _____

14. _____   19. _____

15. _____   20. _____

Spelling Words

1. radiant
2. confident
3. engineer
4. typist
5. electrician
6. inexact
7. outdated
8. downfall
9. upfront
10. upwind
11. admiration
12. addition
13. emotional
14. abdominal
15. testimonial
16. decoration
17. effortlessly
18. meaningfully
19. truthfully
20. carefully

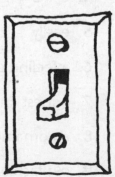

Spelling Practice Book
© Harcourt • Grade 4

Name _____

▶ Read each Spelling Word. Then sort and write them where they belong in the chart.

Words with -ation	Words with -al
1. _____	4. _____
2. _____	5. _____
Word with -ition	Word with -ial
3. _____	6. _____

Spelling Words

1. radiant
2. confident
3. engineer
4. typist
5. electrician
6. inexact
7. outdated
8. downfall
9. upfront
10. upwind
11. admiration
12. addition
13. emotional
14. abdominal
15. testimonial
16. decoration
17. effortlessly
18. meaningfully
19. truthfully
20. carefully

▶ Write the Spelling Word that best completes each analogy.

7. *Serious* is to *comical* as *precise* is to _____.

8. *Track* is to *runner* as *keyboard* is to _____.

9. *Happy* is to *glad* as _____ is to *certain*.

10. *Fast* is to *quickly* as *easily* is to _____.

11. *Pipe* is to *plumber* as *wire* is to _____.

12. *Car* is to *driver* as *train* is to _____.

13. *Joy* is to *joyfully* as *meaning* is to _____.

14. *Downcast* is to *sad* as *happy* is to _____.

15. *Noisily* is to *loudly* as _____ is to *cautiously*.

16. *Dance* is to *gracefully* as *speak* is to _____.

▶ Write the Spelling Word that is similar to the given word.

17. old-fashioned _____   19. honest _____

18. failure _____   20. windward _____

101

Name _____

▶ **Unscramble the syllables to write Spelling Words.**

1. ful ly care   _____

2. mean ful ing ly   _____

3. ef less ly fort   _____

4. ly ful truth   _____

▶ **Perform the math operation to write a Spelling Word.**

5. type – e + ist =   _____

6. abdomen – en + inal =   _____

7. elect + ric + ian =   _____

8. admire – e + ation =   _____

9. decorate – e + ion =   _____

10. confide + nt =   _____

11. emotion + al =   _____

12. add + it + ion =   _____

13. engine + er =   _____

14. radiate – te + nt   _____

15. infant – fant + exact   _____

16. testimony – y + ial   _____

▶ **Match the words to make a Spelling Word. Write each word you make.**

17. up   dated   _____

18. down   up   _____

19. out   fall   _____

20. front   wind   _____

Spelling Words

1. radiant
2. confident
3. engineer
4. typist
5. electrician
6. inexact
7. outdated
8. downfall
9. upfront
10. upwind
11. admiration
12. addition
13. emotional
14. abdominal
15. testimonial
16. decoration
17. effortlessly
18. meaningfully
19. truthfully
20. carefully

Spelling Practice Book

Name _____

▶ **Fold the paper along the dotted line. As each Spelling Word is read aloud, write it in the blank. Then unfold your paper and check your work. Practice writing any Spelling Words you missed.**

1. _____

2. _____

3. _____

4. _____

5. _____

6. _____

7. _____

8. _____

9. _____

10. _____

11. _____

12. _____

13. _____

14. _____

15. _____

16. _____

17. _____

18. _____

19. _____

20. _____

Spelling Words

1. subtle
2. scene
3. climbed
4. comb
5. exhibit
6. doubt
7. folks
8. exhaust
9. half
10. whistle
11. island
12. lamb
13. numb
14. often
15. rustle
16. debt
17. knack
18. thumb
19. unknown
20. mortgage

School–Home Connection

Play "spelling charades" with your child. Take turns using gestures and movements to show each Spelling Word. As each word is guessed, have your child spell the word aloud.

103

Name _____

▶ **Replace the underlined words with Spelling Words.**

Jon has a **(1)** talent for finding odd things. Once, as
he and his father **(2)** hiked up a riverbank, Jon noticed a
(3) slight change in the rocks below. Among the river rocks,
Jon saw an odd object. Since he **(4)** frequently collected
rocks, Jon wanted this one. It was **(5)** partially buried.
After careful digging, he held up a gigantic bone. "I
(6) don't believe this is an ordinary bone," he said.

1. _____   4. _____

2. _____   5. _____

3. _____   6. _____

▶ **Write a Spelling Word to complete each list.**

7. finger, hand, _____

8. setting, picture, _____

9. show, display, _____

10. sheep, ewe, _____

11. brush, hair, _____

12. people, relatives, _____

13. reef, ocean, _____

14. unfeeling, frozen, _____

15. tune, blow, _____

16. flutter, crackle, _____

▶ **Write the following Spelling Words:** *debt, exhaust,*
unknown, **and** *mortgage.* **Use your best handwriting.**

17. _____   19. _____

18. _____   20. _____

Spelling Words

1. subtle
2. scene
3. climbed
4. comb
5. exhibit
6. doubt
7. folks
8. exhaust
9. half
10. whistle
11. island
12. lamb
13. numb
14. often
15. rustle
16. debt
17. knack
18. thumb
19. unknown
20. mortgage

Handwriting Tip

When you write
the letter *u*,
make sure to
bring the last
downstroke to
the bottom line,
or the *u* may be
mistaken for a *v*.

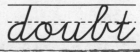

Spelling Practice Book
© Harcourt • Grade 4

▶ **Write a Spelling Word to complete each sentence.**

1. At _____ past twelve, we'll eat lunch.

2. A new museum _____ has come to town.

3. Can you smell the bus engine's _____?

4. Would you like to go to an _____ paradise for vacation?

▶ **Read the directions for sorting below. Then write the Spelling Words.**

Write words that contain a silent *b*.

5. _____   9. _____

6. _____   10. _____

7. _____   11. _____

8. _____   12. _____

Write words that contain a silent *t*.

13. _____   15. _____

14. _____   16. _____

Write words that contain a silent *k*.

17. _____   18. _____

Spelling Words

1. subtle
2. scene
3. climbed
4. comb
5. exhibit
6. doubt
7. folks
8. exhaust
9. half
10. whistle
11. island
12. lamb
13. numb
14. often
15. rustle
16. debt
17. knack
18. thumb
19. unknown
20. mortgage

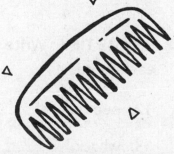

Spelling Strategy

Visualize: If you aren't sure how to spell a word that has a silent letter, picture the word in your mind. Think about the position of the silent letter in the word.

▶ **USE THE CLUES:** Write the Spelling Word that fits each clue. Then unscramble the letters in the boxes to answer the riddle.

1. a home loan □ _ _ _ _ _ _ _ _

2. used to untangle hair _ _ _ _ □ _

3. time and time again _ _ □ _ _ _

4. unfeeling _ □ _ _ _

5. divide in two □ _ _ _

6. What might you say about an amazing finger?

   "Wow, that's some _____!"

Spelling Words

1. subtle
2. scene
3. climbed
4. comb
5. exhibit
6. doubt
7. folks
8. exhaust
9. half
10. whistle
11. island
12. lamb
13. numb
14. often
15. rustle
16. debt
17. knack
18. thumb
19. unknown
20. mortgage

▶ **ANALOGIES:** Write the Spelling Word that best completes each analogy.

7. *Creature* is to *animal* as *people* is to _____.

8. *Plot* is to *action* as *setting* is to _____.

9. *Fireplace* is to *smoke* as *car* is to _____.

10. *Kid* is to *goat* as _____ is to *sheep*.

11. *Fear* is to *bravery* as _____ is to *belief*.

▶ **RHYME TIME:** Write the Spelling Word that rhymes with each word.

12. puddle _____

13. whack _____

14. pet _____

15. puzzle _____

Name _____

▶ Fold the paper along the dotted line. As each Spelling Word is read aloud, write it in the blank. Then unfold your paper and check your work. Practice writing any Spelling Words you missed.

1. _____

2. _____

3. _____

4. _____

5. _____

6. _____

7. _____

8. _____

9. _____

10. _____

11. _____

12. _____

13. _____

14. _____

15. _____

16. _____

17. _____

18. _____

19. _____

20. _____

Spelling Words

1. respect
2. inspect
3. spectacle
4. spectator
5. spectrum
6. specific
7. construct
8. destruction
9. instruct
10. structure
11. autograph
12. photograph
13. phonics
14. telegraph
15. paragraph
16. visor
17. visitor
18. visual
19. visible
20. television

School–Home Connection

Make a list of other words that contain these Greek and Latin word parts: *spect, struct, tele, photo, auto, vis,* and *graph.* Add to the Spelling Word list. Discuss the meaning of each word.

107

Name _____

▶ **Write a Spelling Word to complete each sentence.**

1. I was a _____ to the Grand Canyon.

2. I learned about it from watching a _____ program.

3. We climbed a giant rock _____.

4. From there, the Colorado River was _____.

5. The canyon's cliffs were quite a _____.

6. The layers of rock create a _____ of color.

7. This is a _____ from the trip.

8. I have _____ for the animals there.

9. Since 1919, the Grand Canyon National Park has been protected from _____.

▶ **Write a Spelling Word that is similar to each given word.**

10. teach _____

11. signature _____

12. image _____

13. observer _____

14. build _____

15. particular _____

16. examine _____

▶ **Write the following Spelling Words:** *visor, paragraph, phonics,* **and** *telegraph.* **Use your best handwriting.**

17. _____   19. _____

18. _____   20. _____

Spelling Words

1. respect
2. inspect
3. spectacle
4. spectator
5. spectrum
6. specific
7. construct
8. destruction
9. instruct
10. structure
11. autograph
12. photograph
13. phonics
14. telegraph
15. paragraph
16. visor
17. visitor
18. visual
19. visible
20. television

Handwriting Tip

Be sure to leave enough space between letters so that they are not crowded.

visor

Spelling Practice Book
© Harcourt • Grade 4

Name _____

▶ **Replace the underlined words with Spelling Words.**

Dear Mary,   May 25, 2008

I am sending this **(1)** message to inform you that I am at the Grand Canyon. Truly, this place commands **(2)** admiration! Cliffs are **(3)** observable all around me. I also saw a **(4)** building that was built by people who lived here long ago. Maybe someday you will be a **(5)** guest here, too. Until then, I will send you a **(6)** picture.

Your friend,

John

1. _____	4. _____
2. _____	5. _____
3. _____	6. _____

Spelling Words

1. respect
2. inspect
3. spectacle
4. spectator
5. spectrum
6. specific
7. construct
8. destruction
9. instruct
10. structure
11. autograph
12. photograph
13. phonics
14. telegraph
15. paragraph
16. visor
17. visitor
18. visual
19. visible
20. television

▶ **Write these Spelling Words in alphabetical order.**

television	paragraph	spectrum
phonics	spectacle	visor

7. _____	10. _____
8. _____	11. _____
9. _____	12. _____

▶ **Write the Spelling Word that is the opposite of each given word.**

13. destroy _____   15. preservation _____

14. general _____   16. player _____

Spelling Strategy

Root Words: When you are writing a word with Greek or Latin word parts, identify the root and any prefixes or suffixes. Then think about the meaning of each part.

Spelling Practice Book
© Harcourt • Grade 4

Name _____

▶ **WORD WEBS:** Complete each web with Spelling Words that contain word parts.

1. _____

2. _____

graph to write

3. _____

4. _____

5. _____

6. _____

struct to build

7. _____

8. _____

9. _____

10. _____

vis = to see

11. _____

12. _____

13. _____

Spelling Words

1. respect
2. inspect
3. spectacle
4. spectator
5. spectrum
6. specific
7. construct
8. destruction
9. instruct
10. structure
11. autograph
12. photograph
13. phonics
14. telegraph
15. paragraph
16. visor
17. visitor
18. visual
19. visible
20. television

▶ **WORD SCRAMBLE:** Unscramble each group of letters to write a Spelling Word.

14. scnhoip _____

15. ttocepasr _____

16. ptnisce _____

17. treescp _____

18. mtucerps _____

Spelling Practice Book
© Harcourt • Grade 4

Name _____

▶ Fold the paper along the dotted line. As each Spelling Word is read aloud, write it in the blank. Then unfold your paper and check your work. Practice writing any Spelling Words you missed.

1. _____
2. _____
3. _____
4. _____
5. _____
6. _____
7. _____
8. _____
9. _____
10. _____
11. _____
12. _____
13. _____
14. _____
15. _____
16. _____
17. _____
18. _____
19. _____
20. _____

Spelling Words

1. there
2. they're
3. their
4. sent
5. scent
6. hour
7. our
8. seam
9. seem
10. plain
11. plane
12. piece
13. peace
14. two
15. too
16. to
17. whole
18. hole
19. pail
20. pale

School–Home Connection

Have your child make two sets of index cards with the Spelling Words. Then arrange the cards face down. Take turns matching word cards and spelling the word aloud.

111

▶ **Write Spelling Words that best completes the story.**

In 1804, President Thomas Jefferson ___(1)___ Lewis and Clark on a journey from St. Louis ___(2)___ the Pacific coast. Other people went along, ___(3)___. One was Sacagawea, who helped them make ___(4)___ with the Native Americans. One of ___(5)___ goals was to make maps of the country. These maps may ___(6)___ strange, but ___(7)___ full of details. Finally, the group reached the Pacific Ocean. After spending the winter ___(8)___, they traveled back east. The ___(9)___ trip took more than ___(10)___ years.

1. _____
2. _____
3. _____
4. _____
5. _____

6. _____
7. _____
8. _____
9. _____
10. _____

▶ **Write a Spelling Word to complete each phrase.**

11. put a square peg in a round _____

12. an extra _____ of pizza

13. the sweet _____ of roses

14. sixty minutes in an _____

15. keep it _____ and simple

16. a _____ of water

▶ **Write the following Spelling Words:** *our, seam, plane,* **and** *pale.* **Use your best handwriting.**

17. _____
18. _____

19. _____
20. _____

Handwriting Tip

Make sure the letter *l* touches the top line. Otherwise, it might look like an *e.*

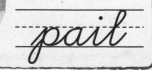

pail

Name _____

▶ **Write the Spelling Word that can replace each underlined word.**

July 22, 1804

It is breakfast time, and I'm watching **(1)** a couple of birds. They **(2)** appear to be eating bugs. They peck at the tree bark and pull insects out of the **(3)** opening. Both have **(4)** light-colored feathers on their chests. They look **(5)** simple and ordinary, but they make a loud tapping sound. For the last **(6)** sixty minutes, I've watched them. Now, it is time to continue our journey.

---

1. _____   4. _____

2. _____   5. _____

3. _____   6. _____

▶ **Write a Spelling Word that has a similar meaning to the given word.**

7. harmony _____

8. also _____

9. entire _____

10. forwarded _____

11. jet _____

12. bucket _____

13. odor _____

14. section _____

15. stitching _____

Spelling Words

1. there
2. they're
3. their
4. sent
5. scent
6. hour
7. our
8. seam
9. seem
10. plain
11. plane
12. piece
13. peace
14. two
15. too
16. to
17. whole
18. hole
19. pail
20. pale

abc Spelling Strategy

Homophones: When you write a word that has a homophone, think about the spellings and meanings of both words. Choose the word that makes sense in your sentence.

Spelling Practice Book
© Harcourt • Grade 4

Name _____

▶ **SOLVE THE PUZZLE:** Write Spelling Words to solve the puzzle. Use the clues to help you.

Spelling Words

1. there
2. they're
3. their
4. sent
5. scent
6. hour
7. our
8. seam
9. seem
10. plain
11. plane
12. piece
13. peace
14. two
15. too
16. to
17. whole
18. hole
19. pail
20. pale

ACROSS
1. ____ a letter
3. Not divided
4. Jack and Jill carried this up a hill
5. Belonging to them
6. Where cloth is joined

DOWN
1. Perfume
2. Period of time
4. A portion or part

▶ **ANALOGIES:** Write the Spelling Word that best completes each analogy.

7. *Down* is to *up* as *from* is to _____.

8. *Her* is to *she* as _____ is to *we*.

9. *I am* is to *I'm* as *they are* is to _____.

▶ **CHOOSE THE WORD:** Circle the Spelling Word that completes each sentence correctly. Then write the word.

10. You look (pail, pale) _____ in the winter.

11. There is a (whole, hole) _____ in that sock.

12. The house is on a flat (plain, plane) _____.

13. Do your friends live on this block or over

    (there, they're) _____?

Spelling Practice Book
© Harcourt • Grade 4

Name _____

▶ Fold the paper along the dotted line. As each Spelling Word is read aloud, write it in the blank. Then unfold your paper and check your work. Practice writing any Spelling Words you missed.

1. _____

2. _____

3. _____

4. _____

5. _____

6. _____

7. _____

8. _____

9. _____

10. _____

11. _____

12. _____

13. _____

14. _____

15. _____

16. _____

17. _____

18. _____

19. _____

20. _____

Spelling Words

1. impatiently
2. disappearance
3. unhappily
4. unnaturally
5. refreshment
6. mistakenly
7. nonrefundable
8. remarkable
9. unlikely
10. unpleasantly
11. disagreement
12. inaccurately
13. incorrectly
14. irreversible
15. repayment
16. uneasily
17. unhealthy
18. unusually
19. misguidance
20. refillable

School–Home Connection

With your child write the Spelling Words on a sheet of paper. Together, underline the prefixes and suffixes. Discuss their meanings.

Spelling Practice Book
© Harcourt • Grade 4

► **Write a Spelling Word to match each mini-definition.**

1. gone from sight _____

2. can be filled again _____

3. food or drink _____

4. not good for you _____

5. cannot get your money back _____

6. cannot be turned around _____

7. paying back money owed _____

8. taken in the wrong direction _____

9. in an unlikable way _____

10. artificially _____

► **Write the Spelling Word that best completes each sentence.**

11. John looked _____ at the sky.

12. The snowstorm was _____ strong.

13. It is _____ that he will return.

14. Stickeen was a _____ dog.

15. He often barked _____.

16. John and I had a _____ about the dog.

► **Write the following Spelling Words:** *uneasily, mistakenly, inaccurately,* **and** *incorrectly.* **Use your best handwriting.**

17. _____   19. _____

18. _____   20. _____

Spelling Words

1. impatiently
2. disappearance
3. unhappily
4. unnaturally
5. refreshment
6. mistakenly
7. nonrefundable
8. remarkable
9. unlikely
10. unpleasantly
11. disagreement
12. inaccurately
13. incorrectly
14. irreversible
15. repayment
16. uneasily
17. unhealthy
18. unusually
19. misguidance
20. refillable

Handwriting Tip

When writing the letter *t*, be sure to cross the *t* clearly and not to loop it.

thy

Name _____

▶ **Unscramble the syllables to write a Spelling Word.**

1. pi hap un ly _____

2. cor in ly rect _____

3. tak ly en mis _____

4. ment re fresh _____

5. gree a dis ment _____

6. pay re ment _____

7. guid ance mis _____

8. mit ad ted re _____

9. ac in cu rate ly _____

10. nat un ur al ly _____

11. ly pleas un ant _____

Spelling Words

1. impatiently
2. disappearance
3. unhappily
4. unnaturally
5. refreshment
6. mistakenly
7. nonrefundable
8. remarkable
9. unlikely
10. unpleasantly
11. disagreement
12. inaccurately
13. incorrectly
14. irreversible
15. repayment
16. uneasily
17. unhealthy
18. unusually
19. misguidance
20. refillable

▶ **Write a Spelling Word to replace the underlined words in each phrase.**

12. the sick animal _____

13. waiting restlessly by the door _____

14. an amazing accomplishment _____

15. surprised by the unexpected outcome _____

Spelling Strategy

Reading Backward: To catch more spelling mistakes, try proofreading backward.
Start with the last word and read until you get to the first. Then read for meaning.

117

Spelling Practice Book
© Harcourt • Grade 4

Name _____

▶ **WORD OPERATIONS: Perform the math operation to write a Spelling Word.**

1. un + happy – y + i + ly = _____

2. mis + take + n + ly = _____

3. un + like + ly = _____

4. ir + reverse – e + ible = _____

5. un + easy – y + i + ly = _____

6. mis + guide – e + ance = _____

7. dis + appeared – ed + ance = _____

▶ **ADD IT ON: Add a prefix and a suffix to each base word to write a Spelling Word.**

8. usual _____

9. pleasant _____

10. refund _____

11. agree _____

12. natural _____

▶ **BREAK THE CODE: Use the code below to write Spelling Words.**

1	2	3	4	5	6	7	8	9	10	11	12	13
A	B	C	D	E	F	G	H	I	J	K	L	M

14	15	16	17	18	19	20	21	22	23	24	25	26
N	O	P	Q	R	S	T	U	V	W	X	Y	Z

13. <u>9</u> <u>13</u> <u>16</u> <u>1</u> <u>20</u> <u>9</u> <u>5</u> <u>14</u> <u>20</u> <u>12</u> <u>25</u> _____

14. <u>18</u> <u>5</u> <u>6</u> <u>18</u> <u>5</u> <u>19</u> <u>8</u> <u>13</u> <u>5</u> <u>14</u> <u>20</u> _____

15. <u>9</u> <u>14</u> <u>1</u> <u>3</u> <u>3</u> <u>21</u> <u>18</u> <u>1</u> <u>20</u> <u>5</u> <u>12</u> <u>25</u> _____

Spelling Practice Book
© Harcourt • Grade 4

Name _____

▶ Write the missing silent letter to complete each Spelling Word. Then write the word.

1. de __ t   _____

2. num __   _____

3. rus __ le   _____

4. s __ ene   _____

5. __ nack   _____

▶ Write the Spelling Word that is the opposite of each word.

6. received   _____

7. dark   _____

8. correctly   _____

9. normally   _____

▶ Change one or two letters in each word to write a Spelling Word.

10. do   _____   13. ewe   _____

11. zoo   _____   14. laid _____

12. spent _____

▶ Write a Spelling Word to complete each set.

15. instruct, construction, _____

16. phonograph, telephone, _____

17. paying, payable, _____

18. guide, guideline, _____

19. specify, species, _____

20. graph, autograph, _____

Spelling Words

1. scene
2. numb
3. rustle
4. debt
5. knack
6. specific
7. phonics
8. destruction
9. paragraph
10. sent
11. scent
12. pail
13. pale
14. to
15. too
16. two
17. inaccurately
18. unusually
19. repayment
20. misguidance

Spelling Practice Book
© Harcourt • Grade 4

▶ **Unscramble the syllables to write Spelling Words.**

1. ics   phon   _____

2. a   graph   par   _____

3. ci   spe   fic   _____

4. tion   de   struc   _____

▶ **Answer each riddle with a Spelling Word that rhymes.**

5. Conceal a view   Screen a _____

6. A cold digit   A _____ thumb

7. Money owed a pet doctor   A _____ to the vet

8. A man's perfume   A _____ for a gent

9. Weigh a bucket   Put the _____ on the scale

10. Make a second cup of tea   Brew for _____

11. When you're sick also   "I have the flu, _____."

▶ **Add the Spelling Words to complete the word chain.**

Spelling Words
1. scene
2. numb
3. rustle
4. debt
5. knack
6. specific
7. phonics
8. destruction
9. paragraph
10. sent
11. scent
12. pail
13. pale
14. to
15. too
16. two
17. inaccurately
18. unusually
19. repayment
20. misguidance

m		s		u					e	
			k				p			
	t									o
	i				r		e		y	
		k							
		y							

Spelling Practice Book
© Harcourt • Grade 4

Name _____

▶ **Write the Spelling Word that fits each clue.**

1. mailed _____

2. in addition or also _____

3. light-colored _____

4. toward _____

5. one less than three _____

6. a bucket _____

7. an odor or fragrance _____

8. shows a place _____

9. to move about _____

10. several related sentences _____

11. rhymes with thumb _____

12. very exact _____

13. study of letters and sounds _____

Spelling Words

1. scene
2. numb
3. rustle
4. debt
5. knack
6. specific
7. phonics
8. destruction
9. paragraph
10. sent
11. scent
12. pail
13. pale
14. to
15. too
16. two
17. inaccurately
18. unusually
19. repayment
20. misguidance

▶ **Write the Spelling Word that best completes each analogy.**

14. *Lead* is to *mislead* as *guidance* is to

_____.

15. *Easy* is to *simple* as _____ is to *talent*.

16. *Construction* is to *build* as _____ is to *tear down*.

17. *Pay* is to *bill* as *owe* is to _____.

18. *Incorrectly* is to *correct* as _____ is to *accurate*.

19. *Often* is to *frequently* as *seldom* is to _____.

20. *Develop* is to *redevelopment* as *pay* is to _____.

Name _____

▶ **Unscramble the letters to write a Spelling Word.**

1. ynteepram   _____

2. calytcrnaiue   _____

3. sulaynulu   _____

4. gidecnamsiu   _____

▶ **Rearrange the syllables to write two Spelling Words.**

ics le rust phon   5. _____

6. _____

cif graph spe par a ic   7. _____

8. _____

▶ **Use Spelling Words to solve the puzzle.**

ACROSS
10. faded
12. damage
15. knick-____
17. in the direction of
18. loss of feeling
19. me, ____

DOWN
9. delivered
11. bucket
13. where action occurs
14. odor
16. something owed
17. one, ____, three

Spelling Words

1. scene
2. numb
3. rustle
4. debt
5. knack
6. specific
7. phonics
8. destruction
9. paragraph
10. sent
11. scent
12. pail
13. pale
14. to
15. too
16. two
17. inaccurately
18. unusually
19. repayment
20. misguidance

Spelling Practice Book
© Harcourt • Grade 4

Spelling Strategies

Let us show you some of our favorite spelling strategies!

Here's a tip that helps me spell a word. I **say** the word. Then I **picture** the way it is spelled. Then I **write** it!

When I'm learning how to spell a word, the **Study Steps to Learn a Word** are a big help. See page 2.

I think of ways to spell the vowel sounds in a word. Then I **try different spellings** until the word looks right.

When I don't know how to spell a word, I sometimes just take my best **guess**! Then I **check** it in a **dictionary** or a **thesaurus**.

Sometimes I **proofread** a sentence **backward**. I start with the last word and end with the first word. It really helps me notice words I've misspelled! Then I proofread for meaning.

I **proofread** my work **twice**. First, I circle words I know are misspelled. Then, I look for words I'm not sure of.

123

When I write a word that is a **homophone**, I make sure the word makes sense in the sentence.

When I'm writing a **compound word**, I think about how the **two smaller words** are spelled.

Sometimes thinking of a **rhyming word** helps me figure out how to spell a word.

I think about **spelling rules**, such as how to change a word's spelling before adding the ending *-ed* or *-ing*.

Drawing the **shape** of a word helps me remember its spelling. This is the shape of the word *yellow*.

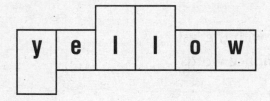

When I **proofread**, I like to **work with a partner**. First, I read the words aloud as my partner looks at the spelling. Then we switch jobs.

Spelling Practice Book
© Harcourt • Grade 4

My Spelling Log

A Spelling Log is a place where you can keep track of words
that are important to you. List words that are new and
interesting on this page. Then list Spelling Words to Study
on pages 126–128.

My Own Word Collection	

Spelling Words to Study

List the words from each lesson that need your special attention.
Be sure to list any words that you misspelled on the Pretest.

THEME 1	THEME 2
Lesson 1: Words with Short Vowels	**Lesson 6:** Words with Consonant *-le*
Lesson 2: Words with Long Vowels and Vowel Digraphs	**Lesson 7:** Words with VCCV: Same Medial Consonants
Lesson 3: Words with Variant Vowels and Diphthongs	**Lesson 8:** Words with VCCV: Different Medial Consonants
Lesson 4: Words with Inflections *-ed* and *-ing*	**Lesson 9:** Words with VCCCV

Spelling Practice Book
© Harcourt • Grade 4

Spelling Words to Study

THEME 3	THEME 4
Lesson 11: Words with VCV	**Lesson 16:** Words Ending with /əl/
Lesson 12: Words with Prefixes *re-, un-, non-*	**Lesson 17:** Words with Ending /ər/
Lesson 13: Words with Suffixes *-able, -ible, -ness, -ment, -less*	**Lesson 18:** Words Parts *over-, under-, sub-*
Lesson 14: Words with Ending /ən/	**Lesson 19:** Words with Irregular Plurals and Possessives

Spelling Words to Study

THEME 5	THEME 6
Lesson 21: Words with Suffixes *-ant, -ent, -eer, -ist, -ian*	**Lesson 26:** Words with Silent Letters
Lesson 22: Word Parts *in-, out-, down-, up-*	**Lesson 27:** Words with Greek and Latin Word Parts
Lesson 23: Words with Suffixes *-ation, -ition, -al, -ial*	**Lesson 28:** Homophones
Lesson 24: Words with Suffixes in Combination	**Lesson 29:** Words with Prefix + Base + Suffix

Handwriting
Manuscript Alphabet

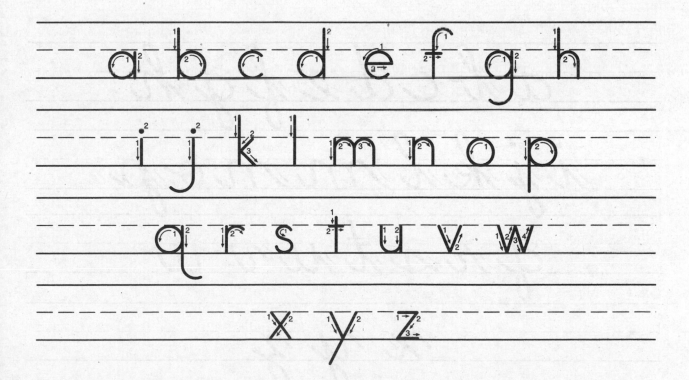

Handwriting

Cursive Alphabet

$\mathcal{A}\ \mathcal{B}\ \mathcal{C}\ \mathcal{D}\ \mathcal{E}\ \mathcal{F}\ \mathcal{G}\ \mathcal{H}$

$\mathcal{I}\ \mathcal{J}\ \mathcal{K}\ \mathcal{L}\ \mathcal{M}\ \mathcal{N}\ \mathcal{O}\ \mathcal{P}$

$\mathcal{Q}\ \mathcal{R}\ \mathcal{S}\ \mathcal{T}\ \mathcal{U}\ \mathcal{V}\ \mathcal{W}$

$\mathcal{X}\ \mathcal{Y}\ \mathcal{Z}$

$a\ b\ c\ d\ e\ f\ g\ h$

$i\ j\ k\ l\ m\ n\ o\ p$

$q\ r\ s\ t\ u\ v\ w$

$x\ y\ z$

Spelling Practice Book
© Harcourt • Grade 4

Handwriting

D'Nealian Manuscript Alphabet

A B C D E F G H

I J K L M N O P

Q R S T U V W

X Y Z

a b c d e f g h

i j k l m n o p

q r s t u v w

x y z

Handwriting

D'Nealian Cursive Alphabet

A B C D E F G H
I J K L M N O P
2 R S T U V W
X Y Z

a b c d e f g h
i j k l m n o p
q r s t u v w
x y z

Spelling Practice Book
© Harcourt • Grade 4